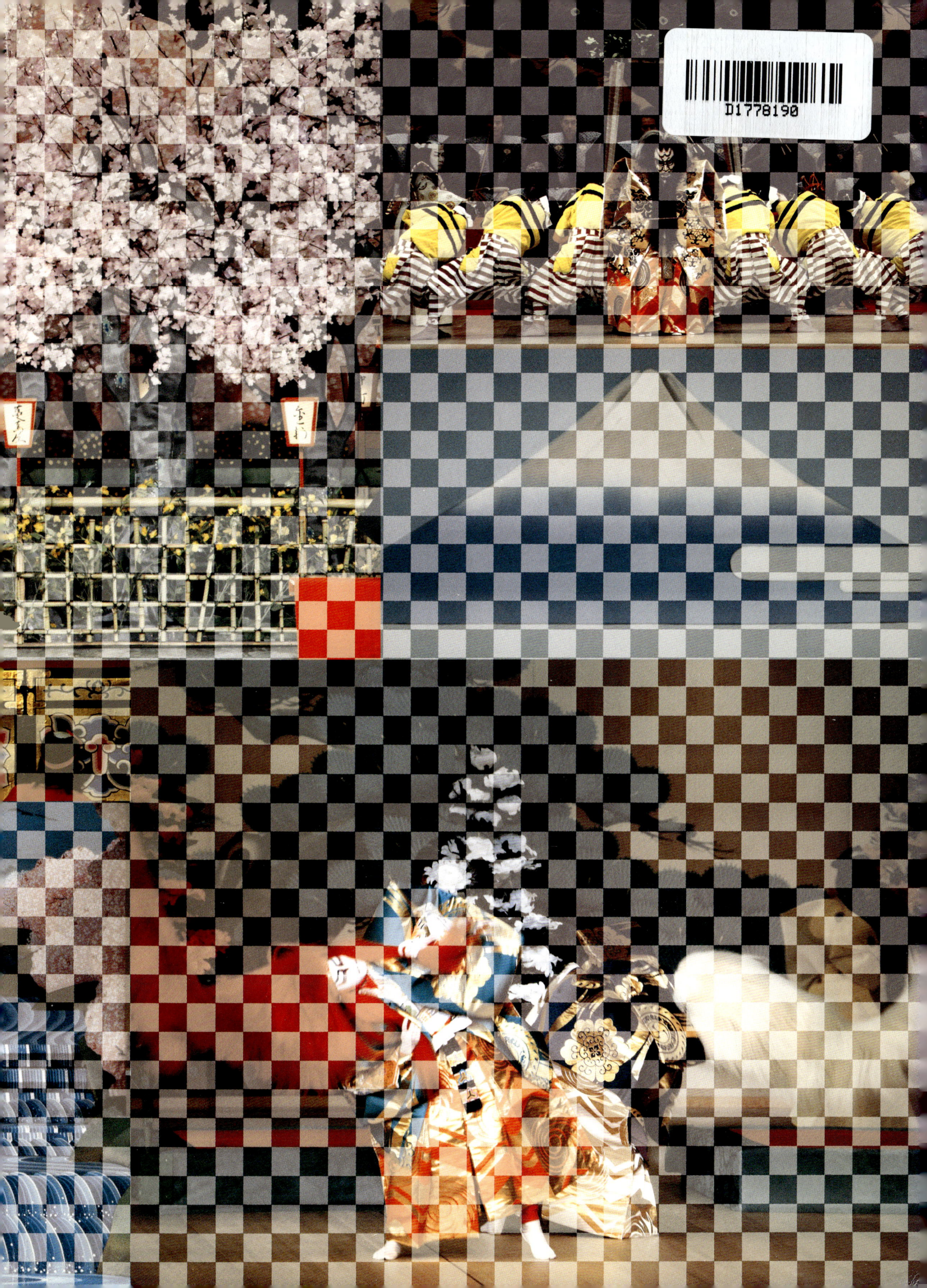

Kabuki Today
The Art and Tradition

Photographs by **Shunji Ohkura**

Introduction by **Donald Keene**
Text by **Iwao Kamimura**
Translated by **Kirsten McIvor**

KODANSHA INTERNATIONAL
Tokyo · New York · London

Photographs by Shunji Ohkura

All photographs in this book were taken with cameras using lenses made by SIGMA Corporation.

Text by Iwao Kamimura.
Translated by Kirsten McIvor. Captions and "About Theater" translated by Shinji Ichiba.
Book Design by Norio Ishiguro.

Editor's Note: Japanese proper names are treated in Japanese style: family name first and given name second. In the captions and list of photographs, actors no longer living as of January 2001 are indicated by generation numbers appearing in conjunction with their names.
Certain plays are illustrated with photographs taken from more than one performance and may thus feature different actors.

Published by Kodansha International Ltd., 17-14, Otowa 1-chome, Bunkyo-ku, Tokyo 112-8652, and Kodansha America, Inc.
Distributed in the United States by Kodansha America, Inc., 575 Lexington Avenue, New York, New York 10022, and in the United Kingdom and continental Europe by Kodansha Europe Ltd., 95 Aldwych, London WC2B 4JF.

Copyright © 2001 by Shunji Ohkura and Kodansha International Ltd. All rights reserved.
Printed in Japan.
First edition, 2001

01 02 03 04   10 9 8 7 6 5 4 3 2 1
ISBN 4-7700-2135-6

Contents

Introduction by Donald Keene——8
本書に寄せて　ドナルド・キーン

What Is Kabuki?——13
歌舞伎とは

Traditions: Inheriting the Art——16
伝統──芸の伝承

***Hanamichi*: The Flower Path**——36
花道

***Kabuki Jūhachiban*: Eighteen Favorite Plays of Kabuki**——42
歌舞伎十八番

Mie* and *Kimari——54
見得ときまり

***Kumadori* Makeup**——58
化粧──隈取

Types of Kabuki Plays——64
狂言の種類

***Tachiyaku*: Male Roles**——126
立役

***Onnagata*: Female Roles**——130
女形

Leading *Onnagata* of Modern Times: Utaemon and Tamasaburō——132
代表する女形　歌右衛門と玉三郎

***Odori*: Kabuki Dance**——146
踊り

Music——150
音楽

Costume: *Bukkaeri*——152
衣装──ぶっ返り

Costume: *Hikinuki*——168
衣装──引抜き

***Hanagata*: The Youngest Generation of Actors**——169
花形　21世紀を彩る若手たち

Kabuki Revitalized——174
歌舞伎に新しい風

List of Photographs——184

Yagō——190

Theaters——191

Introduction

Donald Keene

To say of a performance that it is theatrical is not necessarily a compliment. If said of a European play, it suggests exaggerated, overly realistic depictions of the emotions, and is often contrasted unfavorably with the supposedly superior understatement. If the performance of a Nō actor is praised as excitingly theatrical, he may feel annoyed that the audience was moved not by the transcendent beauty of his singing and dancing but by vulgar theatricality. But Kabuki is above all theatrical. Every element of a performance is exploited to yield the most intense dramatic effects, making a Kabuki performance a supremely theatrical experience.

Of the different varieties of Japanese theatre—Nō, Bunraku, Kabuki and modern drama—Kabuki is the easiest for an audience to admire. The magnificence of the scenery, the costumes of the performers, and the musical accompaniment excite even the most jaded theatregoer. Kabuki unashamedly makes use of even the crudest (as well as the most subtle) theatrical devices to achieve its ends. The Japanese are known for their preference for suggestion and simplicity, as found in their landscape gardening, the tea ceremony, or the Nō theatre, but Kabuki delights in bright colors and the characters who people its stage are apt to be larger than life.

As the play *Shibaraku* starts, the curtain is drawn aside to reveal a crowd of warriors, court ladies, priests, and strongmen dazzlingly arrayed across the wide stage. To emphasize the ferocious strength of the strongmen, their heavily padded bodies are painted brick red, and their faces are boldly decorated. They speak with contemptuous sneers and a rolling of the eyes. But at a cry from the *hanamichi*, the raised passageway through the audience, the people on the stage quiver with fear; even the strongmen who a moment ago defied heaven and earth now cringe in dismay. As we are wondering what has caused this display of terror, a man comes striding along the *hanamichi*. He is dressed in a costume with enormous sleeves that are almost as big as himself, and wears a preposterously big sword. When he stands on the *hanamichi* and berates his enemies with sputtering syllables that go beyond human speech, the audience enjoys a moment that seems like a crystallization of Kabuki.

To a foreign audience, perhaps the most unusual feature of Kabuki is the practice of having the roles of women taken by men known as *onnagata*. This practice originated in the seventeenth century when the government forbade women to appear on the Kabuki stage because of the many fights their charms had inspired among rival admirers. There is no longer a prohibition on actresses in Kabuki, but for most spectators the *onnagata* is an indispensable part of the magic of Kabuki.

The *onnagata* in Kabuki attempts to distill the femininity of his role, hoping that his every gesture or change of expression will convince the audience that he is a woman. Yet the audience never really forgets that he is a man, and this contradiction is the essence of the allure of the *onnagata*. The audience must simultaneously believe and not believe that the actor is a woman. The *onnagata*, aware of the importance of this contradiction to the success of Kabuki, always preserves an element of the unreal in his performance. He models his voice not on the voices of real women but on those of his predecessors, the great *onnagata* of the past. The presence of *onnagata* helps to maintain performances on a high artistic level even when the plays are not of literary distinction.

The plays performed on the Kabuki stage mostly date back to the eighteenth and early nineteenth centuries. They depict traditional Japan before it was affected by Western influence. Such familiar elements of life in the Tokugawa period as the licensed quarters appear in many plays, and the morality has often been termed "feudal," reflecting the ideals of the time. For this reason, during the American occupation of Japan, when it was attempted to extirpate feudalism from Japan, severe restraints were placed on the Kabuki works that might be performed. Fortunately, a member of the occupation, Faubion Bowers, who was passionately devoted to Kabuki, succeeded in getting the ban lifted.

The licensed quarters have disappeared, and few Japanese regulate their lives by feudal principles, but Kabuki goes on. The theatre in other countries has often been called a "mirror of life," but Kabuki is less a mirror than a magnifying glass, enlarging and enhancing life to bring out to the full its color, its excitement, and its theatricality. And, as these marvellous photographs of Kabuki by Ohkura Shuji demonstrate, the pleasures of Kabuki can be appreciated even by those not fortunate enough to have attended a performance.

本書に寄せて　　　　ドナルド・キーン

　ある舞台を見て「芝居みたいだ」と言ったら、これは必ずしも褒め言葉にならない。それがヨーロッパの劇であれば、感情の描写が写実を越えて大げさだと言っているので、より優れた控えめな表現と対照して好ましくないとされることが多い。ある能楽師の舞台を褒めて「芝居のように興奮した」と言えば、能楽師は観客が自分の謡や舞の比類のない美に感動したのでなく、俗っぽい芝居らしさに心動かされたと思って大いに不愉快に感じるかもしれない。しかし歌舞伎は、何にも増して芝居っ気たっぷりである。およそ舞台のあらゆる要素が最高度の劇的効果をもたらすために駆使され、歌舞伎の上演を至高の演劇体験に仕立て上げる。

　日本の様々な演劇形態——能、文楽、歌舞伎、現代劇の中で、その魅力が一番端的でわかりやすいのは歌舞伎である。華麗な舞台装置、役者の衣裳、お囃子（はやし）は芝居を見飽きた観客さえも興奮させてやまない。歌舞伎は、その目的を達成するためなら（繊細な工夫と同時に）けばけばしい演劇的仕掛けをも活用して恥じない。もとより日本人は暗示と簡素を好むことで知られていて、それは日本庭園、茶の湯、能舞台を見ればわかる。しかし歌舞伎は派手な色彩で観客の目を楽しませてくれ、その舞台を動きまわる人物はとかく誇張されがちである。

　歌舞伎十八番の一つ「暫」（しばらく）の幕が開くと、大名、官女、僧侶、武者が、まばゆいばかりに舞台一杯に並んでいる。武者の恐ろしいまでの強さを強調するために、ごてごてと詰め物をした胴体は赤煉瓦色（あかれんがいろ）に塗られ、顔は豪放に隈取りされている。武者たちは、せせら笑いながらしゃべり、両眼をぎょろつかせる。しかし、花道からの「しばらく！」の掛け声に、舞台にいる者たちは恐怖で身震いし始める。ついさっきまで天地をものともせず威勢のよかった武者たちまで、身をすくめて狼狽している。この恐怖の原因は何だろうと訝（いぶか）っていると、一人の男がおもむろに花道に姿を現す。桁はずれに大きい、ほとんど役者の身体と同じくらい大きい袖がついた衣裳を着込み、途方もなく大きな刀を差している。この男が花道に立ち、人間わざとは思えない凄味のあるメリハリの利いたセリフ回しで舞台に居並ぶ者たちを叱り飛ばす時、観客は歌舞伎が結晶化したようなこの瞬間を心ゆくまで楽しむのである。

　外国人の観客にとって歌舞伎の最も珍しい特徴は、女形と呼ばれる

男の役者が女の役を演じることだろう。この慣習は17世紀に始まったもので、当時の幕府が歌舞伎の舞台に女が出ることを禁じたのは、女優の魅力のとりこになった客同士の喧嘩が絶えなかったからだった。もはや歌舞伎に女優が出ることを妨げる禁令はないが、多くの観客にとって女形は歌舞伎の魅力に欠かせない重要な要素となっている。

　歌舞伎の女形は、あらゆる仕種（しぐさ）や表情の変化によって自分が女であることを観客に納得させることを願い、自分が演じる役の女らしさを純化しようと試みる。しかし観客は女形が男であることを一時たりとも忘れるわけではなくて、この矛盾が女形の魅力の本質である。観客は女形が女であると思い、同時にまた思わないでいるに違いない。女形は、この矛盾が歌舞伎の成功にとって重要であると気づいている。だから、常に自分の演技の中に非現実的な要素をとどめておく。声の手本とするのは現実の女の声ではなくて、偉大な女形だった過去の名優の声である。女形の存在は、かりに作品が文学的に傑出したものでなくても、舞台を芸術的に高い水準に維持するのに一役買う。

　歌舞伎の舞台で演じられる作品はほとんどが18世紀、19世紀初期のもので、そこに描かれている世界は西洋の影響を受ける前の伝統的な日本である。徳川時代には生活の一部だった例えば遊廓は数多くの作品に登場するし、作品を支える倫理観は当時の理想を反映して「封建的」と称されるものが多い。このため米軍の日本進駐時代に日本から封建主義を撲滅しようということになった時、歌舞伎の上演に際して厳しい禁止措置が施された。幸いにも進駐軍の中にフォービアン・バワーズがいて、歌舞伎に情熱を抱いていたバワーズは禁止令の解除に成功した。

　すでに遊廓は姿を消し、また自分の生活を封建的な規範で律する日本人もほとんどいない。しかし、歌舞伎は生き続けている。よその国では、よく演劇は「人生を写す鏡」だと言われてきた。しかし歌舞伎は鏡と言うよりは、拡大鏡である。人生を大写しにし、誇張することで人生の彩（いろど）り、興奮、芝居らしさを十二分に発揮させる。そして、この本にまとめられた大倉舜二氏の素晴らしい写真が示しているように、歌舞伎の喜びは実際に舞台を見る幸運に恵まれなかった人々もまた味わうことが出来るのである。

（翻訳・角地幸男）

What Is Kabuki?

Kabuki traces its origins to exactly the same era as Shakespeare. At the beginning of the 17th century, when the legendary Izumo no Okuni was entertaining spectators with her *Kabuki odori* (Kabuki dance) revue at Shijōgawara in Kyoto, then the capital of Japan, Shakespeare's four great tragedies, beginning with *Hamlet*, were opening in rapid succession at the Globe in London. While Okuni is a figure of legend, there is no doubt that people like her initiated the *Kabuki odori* during this era.

Japan at this time was emerging from what became known as the Warring States period, which had continued for over a century, and was looking forward to a new and more peaceful age under the Tokugawa Shogunate. As a result of the long period of conflict among the *daimyō*, the feudal lords, some members of society faded into obscurity, while others rose to prominence. The social structure of Japan was changing dramatically, and people were seeking new values and new aesthetics. The final years of the Warring States period coincided with the opening up of new trade routes by Europeans, bringing people from nations such as Portugal, Holland, and England to Japan, and with them the various accoutrements of a different culture, including Christianity, guns, glass, and tobacco.

In Japan this culture was dubbed *namban bunka*, the "culture from the southern seas," and one of these cultural imports was an instrument known as a *jabisen*, which entered Japan via the Ryūkyū Islands (Okinawa). The *jabisen*, which consisted of a snakeskin stretched over the box of the instrument, its three strings played using a plectrum, was a string and, at the same time, a percussion instrument, and its new and unusual timbre captured the hearts of the Japanese public as they entered this new age. In Japan there are no large snakes, so the *jabisen* was adapted for Japanese use by substituting cat skin, and strings of twisted silk. This new instrument was used to accompany the *Kabuki odori*, and through this association became Japan's best known instrument, the *shamisen*.

The word "Kabuki" is composed of the three elements that comprise the dramatic form of Kabuki: *ka* for music, *bu* for dance, and *ki* for play or player. However, the actual origin of the word may be found in a homonym, *kabuku* or *kabuki*, meaning to incline or tilt. "Kabuki" means therefore a desire not to remain secure within the constraints of the orthodox, but to seek change.

Kabuki has in fact undergone considerable change in four hundred years. The *Kabuki odori* of Izumo no Okuni was very different from the Kabuki we watch today. For a start Okuni was a woman, while in Kabuki even now the female roles are played by men, the *onnagata*. This is because around a quarter of a century after Okuni's performances the authorities banned women from acting. Men took over all the roles in Kabuki, which led to the emergence of a special kind of artiste known as the *onnagata*. These men sought ways to bring depth and beauty to their portrayals of female characters, from both a technical and a psychological perspective, and with practice created a unique style of acting of which only the *onnagata* was capable. At the same time Kabuki moved from the *Kabuki odori* revue, which relied on the beauty of young women to attract audiences, to the Kabuki that is familiar to us now, with its unique repertoire of varied and complex stories. All the characteristic elements we associate with Kabuki today—the roles and techniques of expression, that is costumes, makeup, scenery, and elements of theater construction—were in this way developed and handed down and new innovations added over many generations. From a holistic perspective, Kabuki is the product of the knowledge and ingenuity of countless people, not only actors but musicians, writers, artisans working behind the scenes, and generations of audiences.

Thus the torch of life that burned in the embryonic *Kabuki odori* of Izumo no Okuni—that is, a longing for the "new and unusual" and a fluid spirit—still burns within Kabuki as its vital essence.

歌舞伎とは

　歌舞伎の起源は、シェイクスピアとまさに同時代である。出雲の阿国と呼ばれる伝承上の女性が、当時日本の首都であった京都の四条河原で、「かぶき踊り」と称する一種のレビューを興行した17世紀初頭、ロンドンのグローブ座では『ハムレット』以下の四大悲劇が次々と初演されていたのである。阿国という女性自体は伝承上の存在だが、彼女に象徴される人物が、この時代に「かぶき踊り」を始めたことは間違いない。

　当時の日本は、百年余にわたって続いていた戦乱の時代がようやく終息し、徳川幕府による新しい、平穏の時代が始まろうとしている時期だった。大名間の争いが長く続いた結果、ある者は没落しある者はのし上り、社会は大きく変動し、新しい価値観や美意識が求められていた。ちょうど戦乱の時代の末頃、ヨーロッパでは新航路が開発され、ポルトガル、オランダ、イギリスなどの人々が日本にまでやって来て、キリスト教、鉄砲、ガラス、タバコなどさまざまな異文化の品々をもたらした。日本ではその異文化を「南蛮文化」(南の海から伝えられた文化)と呼んだが、そのひとつに、琉球(沖縄)を経由して伝えられた蛇皮線という楽器があった。胴に蛇の皮を張り、三本の弦を撥で弾いて演奏するその楽器は、弦楽器であると同時に、一種の打楽器でもあり、その新奇な音色は、新しい時代を迎えようとしていた日本の人々の心を魅了した。大きな蛇のいない日本では、猫の皮を張り、弦は絹糸を縒り合わせるように日本化され、この新しい楽器は「かぶき踊り」の伴奏に使われることによって、以後、日本の最も代表的な楽器として生まれ変わった。

　「歌舞伎」という言葉は、「歌」＝ music、「舞」＝ dance、「伎」＝ play または player という、歌舞伎を構成する三つの要素を組み合わせたものだが、語源からいえば、「傾く」または「傾き」という同音の別の言葉から来ている。「傾き」とは、正統の中に安住せず、流動する心、という意味である。

　事実、400年の間に歌舞伎は随分と変化した。出雲の阿国のかぶき踊りは、現在見る歌舞伎とはかなり違うものである。そもそも、阿国は女性だが、現在の歌舞伎では、女の役も「女形」と称する男優が演じる。これは、阿国から四半世紀ほど後に、幕府の命令で女優が禁じられたためである。歌舞伎にたずさわる者達は、代わりにすべての役を男優だけで演じることにし、女形という専門の技芸者を生み出し、技術的にも精神的にも、男性がいかにして女性の役を深く、美しく演じるかを研究し、実践を積み重ね、女形という男優でなければ表現の出来ない、独特の演技を創造したのである。またそれと共に、若い女性の美しさに頼っていたレビューである「かぶき踊り」から、多彩で複雑なストーリーを持った、独特のドラマツルギーを備えた「歌舞伎」を創り出したのだった。今日の歌舞伎にまで伝わっている、歌舞伎独特の役柄とその表現法(演技の仕方)、衣裳、化粧、舞台装置、劇場の構造、といった、さまざまな、いかにも歌舞伎らしい特徴的な要素は、すべて、こうして幾世代かかって開発され、伝えられ、また新たな工夫を加えつつ、作り上げられたものである。それは、トータルに見れば、俳優だけでなく、興行者、作者、裏方の職人たちから、さらには幾世代もの観客たちをも含めた、無数の人々の知恵と工夫の結晶なのだ。

　このように、出雲の阿国の「かぶき踊り」に胚胎していた、「新奇なもの」への憧れや流動する精神といった生命の灯は、いまなお、歌舞伎の本質として、その奥底に灯り続けている。

Traditions: Inheriting the Art

Ichikawa Shinnosuke and Onoe Kikunosuke are two of the youngest stars of the current generation of Kabuki actors. Both are only twenty-three years of age (as of March 2001), but already they command huge followings.

Ichikawa Shinnosuke and Onoe Kikunosuke are not the first in the Kabuki world, however, to be known by their respective stage names. Shinnosuke is a seventh generation and Kikunosuke a fifth generation Kabuki actor, and the names are those used by their predecessors as young actors. In the case of Shinnosuke, his father Danjūrō was the sixth Shinnosuke, and in that of Kikunosuke, his father Kikugorō was the fourth Kikunosuke. The stage names of Kabuki actors are, in fact, passed down from father to son to grandson. If an actor has no sons to carry on the name, he adopts a youth he considers to have the right qualities and passes the name on to him. Why do they do this? Because the mission of the Kabuki actor is to inherit an acting tradition and bequeath it to those who follow him.

In the case of Shakespearean actors, there has never been, and it is inconceivable there could ever be, for example, a tenth generation Kean or a second generation Olivier. Only the actual works of Shakespeare live on, and the most memorable performances of the most famous actors become no more than a moment in history with the passing of those actors. In contrast, the life force of Kabuki is handed down and lives on through the "art" of the actors, much like the Olympic flame.

It would be a mistake to think of all this in mystical terms. To do so may lead us to see things in Kabuki that are not really there or, conversely, to acquire a mistaken understanding of Kabuki as a unique community bound by old-fashioned conventions. Kabuki actors are members of modern society, who like the average modern Japanese sit in a chair at a table and eat Western food, wear Western clothing, drive cars, and surf the Internet. These actors are modern men who command their "flesh and blood" to perform Kabuki in front of modern audiences, in modern theaters (albeit theaters carefully designed not to look modern). We must not forget that this is Kabuki as we see it today, part of our modern world.

This being the case, why do modern Kabuki actors perpetuate the "convention" of *shūmei*, or passing on a stage name, a convention with its origins in the feudal era? Because, as already mentioned, inheriting an acting tradition from their predecessors, building on it in their own generation, and bequeathing it to the next is the mission of the Kabuki actor, and inheriting and passing on a name with that artistic tradition is the most certain way to achieve this. In this sense, it is more appropriate to think of *shūmei* as a tradition than as a convention.

The name Ichikawa Danjūrō is now being used by the twelfth actor to take the title. This family name was imbued with special significance in Edo Kabuki. This is because around three hundred years ago, during an epoch-making period which saw the formation of Genroku Kabuki (the prototype of Kabuki much as it is today), the first Danjūrō devised an acting technique known as *aragoto* (literally "rough business"), which was to form the basis of Edo Kabuki. Since then, successive generations of actors with the name Danjūrō have maintained and passed on the *aragoto* acting tradition, at the same time contributing to Kabuki as central figures in its development in their own age. Of particular note was Danjūrō IX, who in the latter half of the 19th century pushed actively for the modernization of Kabuki during the turmoil that accompanied Japan's move from the feudal system of the Tokugawa Shogunate to the structure of a modern state. As a result the Kabuki of old was swept away and replaced by an art form adapted to the sensibilities and level of understanding of audiences in a new age.

Onoe Kikugorō is the seventh actor to go by the name Kikugorō. It is an important name—as pivotal to the Kabuki of the Edo period as the name Danjūrō and the *aragoto* acting style—which belongs to a line of actors who made a major contribution to the modernization of Kabuki, and is directly linked to the Kabuki of today. Actors taking the name Kikugorō have always been accomplished performers of urbane and sophisticated realism, skillfully portraying the emotional life and aesthetic sensibilities of the townspeople of Edo in a type of play known as *sewamono*, or "domestic" play, depicting the life of the streets. During the Meiji period in the second half of the 19th century the fifth Kikugorō emerged in friendly rivalry with the ninth Danjūrō, and together the actors were dubbed "Dan-Kiku." Kikugorō's son Kikugorō VI, as well as inheriting and developing his father's art, received special training from Danjūrō IX as the actor chosen by him to take Kabuki into the next era, not only absorbing the classic acting techniques, but also inheriting the task of modernizing Kabuki that was Danjūrō's objective. Kikugorō VI was a brilliant actor of outstanding technical skill and a huge star, and until his death directly after World War II was at the forefront of Kabuki in the first half of the 20th century. His influence was immense, and it would be fair to say that there is hardly a Kabuki actor even today who has not been influenced by the work of Kikugorō VI.

Of course, in saying this we must not forget Nakamura Utaemon, another great actor who with Danjūrō and Kikugorō left his mark on modern Kabuki, or the many other famous figures like Nakamura Kanzaburō, Ichimura Uzaemon, and Morita Kanya from the families of the *Edo San-za* or "three Edo theaters of old" (the Nakamura-za, Ichimura-za, and Morita-za, the three major theaters given special permission for Kabuki performances by the shogunate), and it goes without saying that each era has had many of its own stars. And there is more to Kabuki than the Kabuki of Tokyo (Edo). Kabuki was popular in the former capital of Kyoto and in the financial and commercial center of Osaka, and it is important to remember that Kabuki originally developed in the two major cultural spheres of Edo (Tokyo) and *kamigata* (Kansai) like two wheels of a vehicle, each influencing the other as they progressed.

In households with a family tradition of Kabuki acting, as soon as a boy reaches the age at which he knows what is going on around him he is put on the stage. There is no fixed age for this debut, but as most actors start at six or seven their first roles are not particularly demanding. The leading families such as the Ichikawas and Onoes may even add a special act to the program as the child's debut, for his *ohirome no kōjō* or first words on the stage. When the current Kikunosuke took the stage for the first time at the age of six under his childhood name of Ushinosuke, he played the part of Ushiwakamaru, the young Minamoto no Yoshitsune, hero of twelfth century history and legend, and was joined on stage by his father Kikugorō VII and grandfather and famous *onnagata* the seventh Onoe Baikō, a happy and auspicious debut with three generations of actors directly related on stage together. Shinnosuke made his stage debut at the age of seven, performing with his father Danjūrō XII in "Uirōuri" (The Salve Vendor, one of the *Kabuki jūhachiban* or "Eighteen Favorite Plays of Kabuki" compiled by Danjūrō VII in the 19th century).

After growing up and assuming his adult name, Kikunosuke gave a brilliant performance as the young thief Benten Kozō, a role which has been in the Onoe family for five generations since 1862. Shinnosuke for his part has very recently (January 2000), at the unusually young age of twenty-two, given a marvelous portrayal of Sukeroku, the most important role in the Ichikawa family and one that has been handed down for 287 years, creating a Kabuki boom in the process.

As these examples show, in many cases an actor will have a series of names, starting with a childhood name, another taken as an adult, and yet a third when he becomes the head of the family. For example, the person destined to head the Onoe family makes his debut and spends his childhood with the name of Ushinosuke, becoming Kikunosuke as he grows a little older, and when he finally becomes head of the family he is known as Kikugorō. In the same way, the current Danjūrō started his career as Shinnosuke and was then known as Ebizō before finally taking the name Danjūrō XII.

The custom of changing names in the transition from childhood to maturity was originally a tradition of the warrior class, and the custom of giving successive generations the same name is thought to be in imitation of the great merchant houses of the past such as Kōnoike and Sumitomo. No doubt there are those who would criticize the custom as exclusionary and unsuitable for modern times, and undeniably there is an entertainment aspect to the taking of the name. Still, as mentioned earlier, *shūmei* remains the most reliable means of inheriting and bequeathing an acting tradition, and countless examples have proven that inheriting a famous name endows the individual with an awareness and ambition that provide the impetus for his growth and advancement as an actor.

　市川新之助と尾上菊之助は、現在活躍中の歌舞伎俳優たちの中でも最も若い世代に属するスターである。この本が刊行される2001年3月の時点で、二人とも23歳だが、既に絶大な人気を獲得している。

　しかし市川新之助、尾上菊之助という芸名は、歌舞伎界では彼らが最初の名前ではない。新之助は七代目であり、菊之助は五代目であり、それぞれの先代、即ち六代目新之助とは、新之助の父團十郎が、四代目菊之助とは、菊之助の父菊五郎が、それぞれ若い頃に名乗っていた名前である。このようにして、歌舞伎俳優の芸名は、父から子へ、孫へと受け継がれてゆく。(実子がない場合には、その名にふさわしいと思われる素質を持った人物を養子として、伝えてゆく。) 何故このようなことをするのかといえば、歌舞伎俳優にとって、芸を受け継ぎ、伝えてゆくことが使命だからである。

　シェイクスピア俳優の場合、たとえば十代目のキーンとか二代目のオリヴィエなどという存在は、かつても今も、考えられない。生き続けるのはシェイクスピアの作品そのものであり、いかなる名優たちの名演技も、その肉体とともに歴史の瞬間に消えてしまう。だが歌舞伎の生命は、役者の「芸」を通じて、まるで聖火リレーのように受け継がれ、生き続けるのだ。

　もっとも、こういうことをあまり神秘的に考え過ぎるのは、いいことではない。それは、現実の歌舞伎の実体を過大に解釈したり、逆に、古めかしい因習に雁字搦めになった特殊社会のように誤解する因になりかねない。歌舞伎俳優も現代人であり、現代の平均的な日本人と同じように、椅子とテーブルに座って洋食を食べ、洋服を着、自動車を運転し、インターネットを操る人々である。現代人である俳優が、現代人である観客の前で、現代建築である劇場で(内装には意が凝らされているにせよ)、生身の肉体を駆使して歌舞伎を演じる。それが、われわれが目の当りに見ることの出来る、現代に生きている歌舞伎の姿であることを忘れてはいけない。

　ではそれなら何故、封建時代に由来する「襲名」という因習を、現代の歌舞伎俳優たちが続けているのだろうか？　それは、先刻も言ったように、先人から受け継いだ「芸」を、自分の代で実らせ、次の世代へ伝えることが、彼らにとっての使命だからであり、そのためには、名跡と共に芸を受け継ぎ、伝えることが最も確実な方法だからである。そう考える時、それはもはや、「因習」ではなく「伝統」と考える方が、ふさわしいことが判るだろう。

　市川團十郎という名前は、当代の團十郎で十二代を数える。この名跡は、江戸歌舞伎ではとりわけ重要な、特別視されてきた名前だった。何故なら、いまから300年余り前の、「元禄歌舞伎」と呼ばれる、歌舞伎がほぼ今日まで伝わる形態の原型を確立した大きなエポックの時代に、初代の團十郎が、「荒事」という江戸歌舞伎の根元となる演技法を創始したからである。以後、代々の團十郎達は、荒事を守り伝えると同時に、それぞれの時代の歌舞伎の中心的な存在として歌舞伎の発展に寄与してきたが、とりわけ、19世紀後半、徳川幕府の封建体制に代わって日本が近代的な体制の国家に切り替わった激動の時代に、九代目の團十郎が歌舞伎の近代化を積極的に推し進めた。それによって歌舞伎は、古い体質を洗い落とし、新しい時代の観客の感性と理解力に応え得るものに変容したのである。

　尾上菊五郎という名前は、当代の菊五郎で七代目を数える。この名跡も、團十郎の荒事と並んで江戸歌舞伎の中心的な役割を担うと同時に、現代の歌舞伎に直結する、歌舞伎の近代化に大きな貢献をしたという意味で、とりわけ重要な名前と考えられている。もともと、代々の菊五郎は、市井の人々の生活を活写する「世話物」と呼ばれるジャンルで、

伝統——芸の伝承

　江戸の市民の生活感情や美意識を巧みに演じる、都会的に洗練されたリアリズムの芸に長じていたが、19世紀後半の明治期、五代目菊五郎は、九代目團十郎と拮抗する好敵手として活躍し、「團菊」と併称された。その子の六代目菊五郎は、父の芸を継承・発展すると共に、九代目團十郎から次代を託する者として特別な薫陶を受け、古典の骨法を仕込まれると同時に、團十郎が目指していた歌舞伎の近代化という仕事をも引き継いだ。彼は技巧的にも卓越した名優であり、大変な人気スターでもあったので、第二次大戦直後に没するまで、20世紀前半の歌舞伎をリードした。その影響力は甚大で、それ以降、現代に至るまで、直接と間接とを問わず、六代目菊五郎の影響を受けなかった歌舞伎俳優は、ほとんどいないといってもいいほどである。

　もちろん、こうは言っても、團十郎・菊五郎以外にも、近代の歌舞伎に大きな足跡を残したもうひとつの大名跡である中村歌右衛門や、かつての江戸三座（中村座・市村座・守田座。幕府が特に許した三大劇場）の座主の名跡に由来する中村勘三郎・市村羽左衛門、守田勘弥など、大きな名跡は数々あり、その時代その時代の名優たちが多勢いたのは言うまでもない。また、江戸（東京）歌舞伎だけが歌舞伎のすべてではない。かつての首都だった京都、金融と商業の中心だった大阪でも歌舞伎は盛んであり、江戸（東京）と上方と、二つの大きな文化圏で、互いに影響をし合いながら、車の両輪のように展開されてきたのが、本来の歌舞伎の在り方だったことは、忘れてはならない。

　由緒ある家柄の家では、男の子が物心つく年頃になると、初舞台を踏ませる。何歳という決まりはないが、大概6、7歳ぐらいの幼い頃だから、それほど難しい役をするわけではない。市川家や尾上家などの有力な家柄の子の初舞台の折には、その「御披露目の口上」（デビューの挨拶）のための一幕をわざわざ作ることもある。いまの菊之助が、幼名の丑之助を名乗って六歳で初舞台を踏んだ時には、12世紀の歴史上また伝説上の英雄である源義経の幼年時代の牛若丸の役で、父親の七代目菊五郎、祖父の名女形七代目尾上梅幸と、直系の三代が一緒に舞台で顔を合わせるという、ほほえましくも晴れがましいデビューだった。また新之助が初舞台を踏んだのは7歳の時だったが、19世紀に七代目團十郎が制定した「歌舞伎十八番」の中の『外郎売』を、父の十二代目團十郎と共演したのだった。

　やがて成長した菊之助は、その名を襲名する時、1862年より尾上家に五代続く家の芸である弁天小僧を見事に演じた。また新之助は、つい最近（2000年1月）22歳という異例の若さで、市川家に287年伝わる最も大切な役である助六を見事に演じて、一躍ブームを起こした。

　この例からも窺われるように、由緒ある名跡の中には、子供の時に名乗る名前、成長してから名乗る名前、家の当主となって名乗る名前という風に、段階を踏んで次々と襲名してゆくというケースも少なくない。たとえば尾上家の当主になる者は、はじめは幼名の丑之助として初舞台を踏み、子供時代を過ごし、やや成長して菊之助となり、やがて当主となって菊五郎になるわけである。同じように今の團十郎は、はじめ新之助から海老蔵を経て、十二代目を襲ったのだった。

　幼名から成人して名を替えるのは、元々は武家の風習であり、また代々の当主が同じ名を襲名するのは、鴻ノ池、住友などかつての商家の風習に倣ったものと思われる。現代にそぐわない閉鎖的な因習と批判的に見る意見もあろうし、襲名というイベントを興行的に利用するという側面もないとはいえない。しかし先にも言ったように、芸を受け継ぎ伝えるための最も確実な方法という一面と、大名跡を継ぐことにより、本人の自覚と意欲が俳優としての成長・飛躍のスプリングボードとなる効果は、幾多の先例が確実に実証している。

尾上菊之助初舞台

Onoe Kikunosuke during his first stage appearance, age six, as part of the ceremony marking his succession to the name of Ushinosuke (in 1996 he would become Kikunosuke).
Here he is playing the role of Ushiwakamaru in *Ehon Ushiwakamaru* with his father, Onoe Kikugorō VII, in the background. February 1984.

6歳、尾上菊之助初舞台（六代目尾上丑之助襲名）
『絵本牛若丸』の牛若丸、父の尾上菊五郎と（1984年2月、歌舞伎座）

祖父と孫…

Onoe Kikunosuke (Ushinosuke) as Tōmi of Higuchi in *Hirakana Seisuiki*. November 1984.
『ひらかな盛衰記』 遠見の樋口　尾上菊之助（丑之助）（1984年11月、国立劇場）

Onoe Baikō VII, grandfather, as Chiyo, and Onoe Kikunosuke (Ushinosuke), grandson, as Kotarō, in the scene "Terakoya" in *Sugawara Denju Tenarai Kagami*. May 1985.
『菅原伝授手習鑑』の「寺子屋」　千代　七世尾上梅幸　小太郎　尾上菊之助（丑之助）
（1985年5月、歌舞伎座）

Onoe Kikunosuke (Ushinosuke), Bandō Kametoshi (then Masatoshi), and Bandō Kamesaburō as *shoke*, in *Kyōganoko Musume Dōjōji*. March 1985.
『京鹿子娘道成寺』　所化　尾上菊之助（丑之助）、坂東亀寿（正敏）、坂東亀三郎
（1985年3月、国立劇場）

市川家親子二代の襲名

十二代目市川團十郎襲名
七代目市川新之助襲名、初舞台

Ichikawa Danjūrō (XII), father, and Ichikawa Shinnosuke (VII), son, together on stage as part of the ceremony marking their succession to these stage names. Ichikawa Danjūrō as Soga no Gorō, and Ichikawa Shinnosuke, seven-year-old debutant, as Kikanbō, in *Uirō Uri*. May 1985.
市川團十郎　『外郎売』の曽我五郎（1985年5月、歌舞伎座）
7歳、市川新之助初舞台　『外郎売』の貴甘坊（1985年5月、歌舞伎座）

Ichikawa Shinnosuke and Onoe Kikunosuke (Ushinosuke), both ten years old, as *kochō*, in *Kagamijishi*. June 1988.
『鏡獅子』の胡蝶　ともに10歳の市川新之助、尾上菊之助（丑之助）
（1988年6月、歌舞伎座）

Ichikawa Shinnosuke (far left), Onoe Kikugorō, Onoe Kikunosuke (Ushinosuke),
Ichikawa Danjūrō, Sawamura Tanosuke, and Onoe Tatsunosuke (then Sakon), in *Kasane Ōgi Yukari no Ekurabe*. February 1989.
『重扇縁絵競』　左より市川新之助、尾上菊五郎、尾上菊之助（丑之助）、市川團十郎、澤村田之助、尾上辰之助（左近）、（1989年2月、歌舞伎座）

祖父と孫…

Onoe Baikō VII, grandfather, as Masaoka, and Onoe Kikunosuke (Ushinosuke), grandson, as Senmatsu, in *Jitsuroku Sendaihagi*. March 1987.

『実録先代萩』 政岡 七世尾上梅幸 千松 尾上菊之助（丑之助）
（1987年3月、国立劇場）

祖父と孫…

Onoe Baikō VII, grandfather, as Tonase and Onoe Kikunosuke (Ushinosuke), grandson, as Konami, in *Michiyuki Tabiji no Yomeiri*. April 1993.

『道行旅路の嫁入』　戸無瀬　七世尾上梅幸　小浪　尾上菊之助（丑之助）
（1993年4月、明治座）

父と子… Onoe Baikō VII, father, as Otomi, and Onoe Kikugorō, son, as Yosaburō, in *Yowa Nasake Ukina no Yokogushi*. September 1985.
『與話情浮名横櫛』 お富 七世尾上梅幸 与三郎 尾上菊五郎 の共演（1985年9月、郡山市民文化センター）

Onoe Kikugorō, father, as Tonase, and Onoe Kikunosuke, son, as Konami, in the scene "Yamashina Kankyo" in *Kanadehon Chūshingura*. February 1997.
『仮名手本忠臣蔵』の「山科閑居」 戸無瀬 尾上菊五郎 小浪 尾上菊之助（1997年2月、歌舞伎座）

尾上家三代の「道成寺」

Onoe Baikō VII, grandfather, Onoe Kikugorō, son, Onoe Kikunosuke (Ushinosuke), grandson, in *Kyōganoko Musume Sannin Dōjōji*. November 1992.
『京鹿子娘三人道成寺』 七世尾上梅幸、尾上菊五郎、尾上菊之助（丑之助）
（1992年11月、歌舞伎座）

親子二代の「助六」

Ichikawa Danjūrō as Sukeroku, in the ceremony marking his succession to the stage name of Ichikawa Danjūrō (XII). April 1985.
市川團十郎の「助六」(十二代目市川團十郎襲名披露、1985年4月、歌舞伎座)

Ichikawa Shinnosuke, son, as Sukeroku, and Ichikawa Danjūrō, father, as Kampera Mombē. January 2000.
市川新之助の「助六」 市川團十郎の「くわんぺら門兵衛」(2000年1月、新橋演舞場)

親子二代の「弁天小僧」

Onoe Kikugorō as Benten Kozō. April 1993.
尾上菊五郎の「弁天小僧」(1993年4月、明治座)

Onoe Kikunosuke as Benten Kozō. January 2000
尾上菊之助の「弁天小僧」(2000年1月、新橋演舞場)

親子二代の「弁天小僧」

Onoe Kikugorō as Benten Kozō. January 1995.
尾上菊五郎の「弁天小僧」(1995年1月、歌舞伎座)

Onoe Kikunosuke as Benten Kozō. January 2000.
尾上菊之助の「弁天小僧」(2000年1月、新橋演舞場)

Onoe Kikugorō as Benten Kozō. March 1984.
尾上菊五郎の「弁天小僧」(1984年3月、国立劇場)

Onoe Kikunosuke as Benten Kozō. January 2000.
尾上菊之助の「弁天小僧」(2000年1月、新橋演舞場)

菅原伝授手習鑑――車引　Ichikawa Danjūrō as Umeōmaru, and Onoe Kikugorō as Sakuramaru, in the scene "Kuruma-biki" in *Sugawara Denju Tenarai Kagami*. March 2000.
梅王丸　市川團十郎　桜丸　尾上菊五郎（2000年3月、歌舞伎座）

Onoe Tatsunosuke as Umeōmaru, and Onoe Kikunosuke (Ushinosuke) as Sakuramaru, in the scene "Kuruma-biki" in *Sugawara Denju Tenarai Kagami*. May 1993.
梅王丸　尾上辰之助　桜丸　尾上菊之助（丑之助）（1993年5月、歌舞伎座）

Passed on from generation to generation, the art of Kabuki is continually revitalized.

次の世代へと、芸は伝えられ、継がれていく───

本朝廿四孝

Onoe Kikugorō as Takeda Katsuyori, in *Honchō Nijūshi Kō*. March 1999.
尾上菊五郎の武田勝頼（1999年3月、歌舞伎座）

Ichikawa Shinnosuke as Takeda Katsuyori, in *Honchō Nijūshi Kō*. May 2000.
市川新之助の武田勝頼（2000年5月、歌舞伎座）

Hanamichi: The Flower Path

There is more to Kabuki than actors putting on costumes and reciting their lines. Stage devices such as the *hanamichi* (flower path), revolving stage, *seri* (trap lift), and in fact the theater itself are all part of the performance.

The various features of the stage unique to Kabuki were devised and developed in the 18th century, and the creation and development of the acting techniques, costumes, and scripts we see today with their unique aesthetic were in fact closely related to the development of these stage devices. Kabuki is a spatial performance in which all the elements in the space we call the theater participate, from the actors to the scenery, props, and stage devices, and the craftsmen behind the scenes who build and operate them.

The *mawari-butai* (revolving stage) is a circular mechanism cut into the stage, enabling scenes to be changed with the curtain

花道

　歌舞伎とは、ただ俳優が扮装しセリフを言うだけの演劇ではない。花道・廻り舞台・セリといった舞台機構、ひいては劇場そのものまでが芝居に参加しているのだ。

　これらの歌舞伎独特の機構が工夫・開発されたのは18世紀のことだが、歌舞伎の演技や扮装、脚本などが今日見るような、独自の美学のもとに創造され、発達したのは、実はこれらの舞台機構の発達と密接な関係がある。歌舞伎は、俳優、大道具、小道具、舞台機構、それらを作り、操作する裏方の職人たち、劇場という空間の中にあるものすべてが参画して作り上げる、空間のパフォーマンスなのだ。

　廻り舞台は舞台に円盤状にくり抜いた機構で、大道具(舞台装置)ごと、幕を開けたままで場面を転換させることが出来る。セリは、これも舞台に切り抜いた四角い部分で、エレベーター式に上げ下げすることによって、人物が、時には舞台装置ごと、突如出現したり消え失せたりという、超自然的な事象を演出することが出来る。ついでに言えば、幕も、歌舞伎では舞台と客席を仕切るだけでなく、さまざまな用途に応じて大小幾種類もの幕を、局面に応じて使い分け、演出効果を高めるのに役立っている。というより、さまざまな幕もまた、歌舞伎という空間のパフォーマンスに参画しているのだ。

　中でも花道は、歌舞伎の誕生と共にあり、歌舞伎の本質を最もよく象徴する舞台機構といえる。その機能をわざと素っ気なくいえば、人物の登場と退場に使う通路だが、それでは歌舞伎を語ったことにはならない。それは同時に、人物を演じる役者が、劇空間に出、また入る道でもある。助六は、登場するだけのために、20分も曲に合わせて花道でさまざまなポーズをして見せる。『暫』の英雄は、花道で長々と自己紹介のセリフをアリアの如くに朗唱する。また「道行」という旅の情景を舞踊劇に仕立てた一幕では、しばしば、恋人同士が花道を仲良く連れ立って出たり、また入ったりする。観客は、ストーリーの上の人物と、それを演じる役者のスターぶりの双方を、重ね合わせて楽しむ。その二重性。それが歌舞伎の楽しさを解く鍵であり、花道はそれを、客席の中まで貫いて、臨場感と共に満喫させる、もうひとつの舞台なのだ。

open. The *seri* is a square piece also cut into the stage which when raised and lowered like a lift enables supernatural phenomena—such as the sudden appearance and disappearance of people, and sometimes people and scenery—to be shown on stage. The curtain in Kabuki not only separates the stage from the audience, but serves to enhance the impact of the performance via the deployment of a number of curtains large and small for various uses and situations. Or perhaps it would be more accurate to say that these various curtains also play a part in the spatial performance that is Kabuki.

　Of these devices, the *hanamichi* is an original feature of the Kabuki stage, and the one that best symbolizes the characteristics of Kabuki. In the most sparing terms the *hanamichi* could be described as an aisle used by "characters" to appear on and leave the stage. But that would not be doing justice to Kabuki. The *hanamichi* is at the same time a path used by the "actors" who play those characters to enter and exit the space of the theater. Sukeroku takes twenty minutes adopting various poses to music on the *hanamichi* simply to appear. The hero of "Shibaraku" (Wait!) chants a long self-introduction much like an aria on the *hanamichi*. And in "Michiyuki," an act in which a traveling scene is performed as a dance piece, lovers use the *hanamichi* frequently to leave and reappear onstage. The audience enjoys both the "characters" in the story and the star quality of the "actors" who play them. This duality is the key to enjoyment of Kabuki, and the *hanamichi* is another stage that reaches out into the audience, allowing it to experience the performance and the ambience of the theater to the full.

助六由縁江戸桜
Sukeroku Yukari no Edo-zakura

SUKEROKU, FLOWER OF EDO

"Sukeroku" captures the atmosphere of the newly prosperous metropolis of Edo. It is a play, reveling in the world of the dandy, about a tug-of-war between two males over a courtesan in magnificent costume, made even more interesting by the addition of plenty of cursing and fighting. "Sukeroku" is set in the pleasure quarters of Yoshiwara, the world of the fashionable man-about-town, where no man—*samurai* or townsman—is of consequence unless he is popular with the ladies. First and foremost the play gives the audience an opportunity to savor a world of sumptuous luxury, of style and leisure, the world of the fashionable sophisticate of Edo. There is of course a story....

The main character, Sukeroku, is a swashbuckling young fellow who lives by the motto "crush the strong and protect the weak." His lover, Agemaki, is a courtesan in the pleasure quarters, of the highest class of *matsu*. Agemaki can be almost masculine in her caustic rebuttals of the distasteful advances of Sukeroku's rival in love, Hige no Ikyū, and at the same time displays a softer side, protecting Sukeroku like a mother, and empathizing with Sukeroku's mother in her concern for her son's well-being. Ikyū, the *katakiyaku*, or foe, competing with Sukeroku for Agemaki's affections, is an elderly dandy in magnificent white hair and beard.

Sukeroku has a goal: to find the famous lost sword Tomokirimaru and to avenge the death of his father. The sword carried by Ikyū appears to be precisely this sword, and so Sukeroku goads Ikyū into combat....

First staged in 1713. Written by Tsuuchi Jihei. *Jidaimono*.

THE SUBSCRIPTION SCROLL

Kanjinchō 勧進帳

A leading example of the *matsubame* genre of play based on Nō, and one of the works in the *Kabuki jūhachiban* (Eighteen Favorite Plays). "Kanjinchō" is a musical play in three movements that fuses the simplicity of Nō and the drama of Kabuki, and presents them on stage using the lyrical *nagauta* form (in a particularly famous song) to tell the story.

Minamoto no Yoshitsune is an actual figure from history—the younger brother of Minamoto no Yoritomo, who founded the Kamakura Shogunate and established the first warrior government. Yoshitsune, however, is regarded as a tragic figure, a military commander who despite his brilliant success is neglected and banished by his brother, which leads finally to his demise, and various legends surround his life. Exiled by Yoritomo, he flees the capital with a few trusted confidants. Disguised as itinerant priests, they set off in early spring on a clandestine journey to the north. On the way they encounter Togashi Saemon, who guards the barrier at Ataka.

In a daring plan Yoshitsune pretends to be their porter, and Benkei, their leader and a man of both wisdom and courage, responds skillfully to the persistent questioning of Togashi, who suspects that the band are not real priests. For a moment it looks as if Yoshitsune's cover is about to be blown....

Courageous Benkei uses all means at his disposal to protect the melancholy young noble Yoshitsune from discovery. Sensing his distress, Togashi demonstrates the compassion of the warrior by letting them pass, despite realizing Yoshitsune's true identity.

First staged in 1840. Written by Namiki Gohei III. *Nagauta* dance-drama.

53

Mie and Kimari

Anyone who has seen the musical "Lion King" that has been in the news of late will have noticed the bold and effective use of techniques from Kabuki and Bunraku. Many theaters around the world today have revolving stages, and there are numerous similar instances of Kabuki acting techniques and presentation influencing other types of theater.

The stop motion technique used in film is said to have been inspired by the *mie* or poses of Kabuki. Filmmakers were drawn to the effect of bringing time temporarily to a halt. If we think of the *mie* as a full stop or period, then the *kimari* is a comma. As the actor plays his part he takes a single breath at a strategic point, poses, and is still. In other words, he *kimaru* or "settles." *Mie* may be thought of as an expanded version of the *kimari*, with extra emphasis.

Another element of *mie* is to *niramu* or glare. This would not work in film—this "glaring" is a pose unique to Kabuki, closely connected to the *aragoto* style of acting. Statues of the *fudō myō-ō* (God of Fire) and *kongō rikishi* (Deva King) at temples stand still and steadfast with eyes wide, glaring at the demons in what must surely be the original *mie*. In other words, a "sense of power" is the third requisite for a *mie*. Surface tension causes water in a container filled to the brim to be still for a moment. Think of the *mie* as that moment. Naturally *mie* are not used by *onnagata* or *nimaime* (male lover roles) as an expression of strength; these characters only *kimaru*.

最近評判になったミュージカル『ライオンキング』を観た人なら、歌舞伎や文楽の手法が大胆に取り入れられ、効果をあげていることに気がつくだろう。廻り舞台も、今日では、世界の多くの劇場に設けられている。このように、歌舞伎の演技・演出が、他ジャンルの演劇に影響を及ぼした例は少なくない。

映画のストップモーションという手法は「見得」からヒントを得て考え出したのだといわれている。時間を堰きとめる、という効果に着目したのである。見得をフルストップ（ピリオド）とすれば、コンマに相当するのが、「キマリ」である。役者が演技をしながら、要所要所でほんの一呼吸、ポーズをとって静止する。つまり、「キマる」。見得はその「キマリ」を拡大・強調したものと思えばよい。

見得のもうひとつの要件は「睨む」ということにある。これは映画には取り入れるわけにはいかなかった。「睨む」ことは、荒事と密接な関係のある、歌舞伎ならではの行為だからである。不動明王や金剛力士の像は、力がこもって静止した形で大きく目を剥いて悪鬼を睨みつけているが、あれこそまさに「見得」の原形だろう。即ち「力感」ということが、見得の第三の要件である。器に一杯に張った水が表面張力で一旦静止する。その瞬間だと思えばよい。力の表現だから、女形や二枚目（色男役）は、当然のように見得をしない。キマル、だけである。

見得とききまり

鳴神 Narukami

NARUKAMI THE PRIEST

The current version of this work is the one revived about a century ago, although the original dates back some two hundred and fifty years. A high priest ordained by the emperor of the time transgresses his vows when faced with the charm of a beautiful woman, discovers he has been tricked, and flies into a violent rage. Simple and humorous in the style of the legends of old, the story is brought to life on stage in a manner only possible in Kabuki.

Angry at the disorder in the world, the priest Narukami retreats to the furthest reaches of the capital, the northern mountains, to practice religious austerities, and traps a dragon god at the foot of a waterfall. The result is a drought, and the court, fearing the mutterings of the farmers, dispatches the greatest beauty of the palace, the princess Kumo no Taema-hime, to the scene. (The princess's name means "a break in the rain clouds"; in other words, a break between rain and sunshine.) Blessed with both beauty and intelligence, she tells the priest a charming love story, opening up and finally melting the heart of a man who has not known the love of a woman since his mother's breast.

Having broken his vows, the priest changes his wig onstage, redoes his makeup, and is transformed from a high priest into a creature that is the very embodiment of rage. He chases the princess, acting in *aragoto* style as a manifestation of his anger. The *hikinuki*, the pulling off of the priest's costume, symbolizes this change in his personality. The scene in which the dragon god is shown flying up into the sky amid pouring rain and lightning is of particular interest in terms of presentation.

First staged in 1742. Written by Tsuuchi Hanjūrō. *Jidaimono*.

Kumadori Makeup

Kabuki actors wear various kinds of makeup depending on the role. The usual name for the part of the handsome lover is the *shironuri*, or "white face," while that of an official is the *akattsura*, or "red face." Examples of the makeup techniques unique to these roles came to represent the roles themselves.

In Kabuki, all actors apart from the very young apply their own makeup. Makeup is also part of the actor's "art," and there are even roles in which actors change their makeup on stage.

Kumadori, the makeup technique used for *aragoto* roles, like *hanamichi*, *onnagata*, and *mie* (poses) serves as a type of code evoking images of Kabuki in the minds of the general public. In actual fact, *kumadori* is only one of various makeup techniques used in Kabuki, and is only for specific roles. (Thus, it is not at all unusual to sit in a Kabuki audience all day without seeing a single role in *kumadori*.)

Kumadori is undoubtedly a makeup technique born of Kabuki and symbolic of Kabuki. In particular, the *beniguma* technique in which red (*beni*) is used to draw around the eyes, is linked to the *aragoto* style of performance, symbolizing the role of the righteous hero with superhuman powers. The *nihonguma* of the hero of "Shibaraku" is a good example of this kind of makeup, and even among the same *beniguma* the "*mukimi*" *guma* used for Sukeroku and Soga no Gorō marks them as "youthful heroes." "Kuruma-biki" is only a short act serving as a kind of interlude in the lengthy masterpiece "Sugawara Denju Tenarai Kagami" (Sugawara's Secrets of Calligraphy), but with all the main characters in *kumadori*, it is a veritable showcase of this makeup technique.

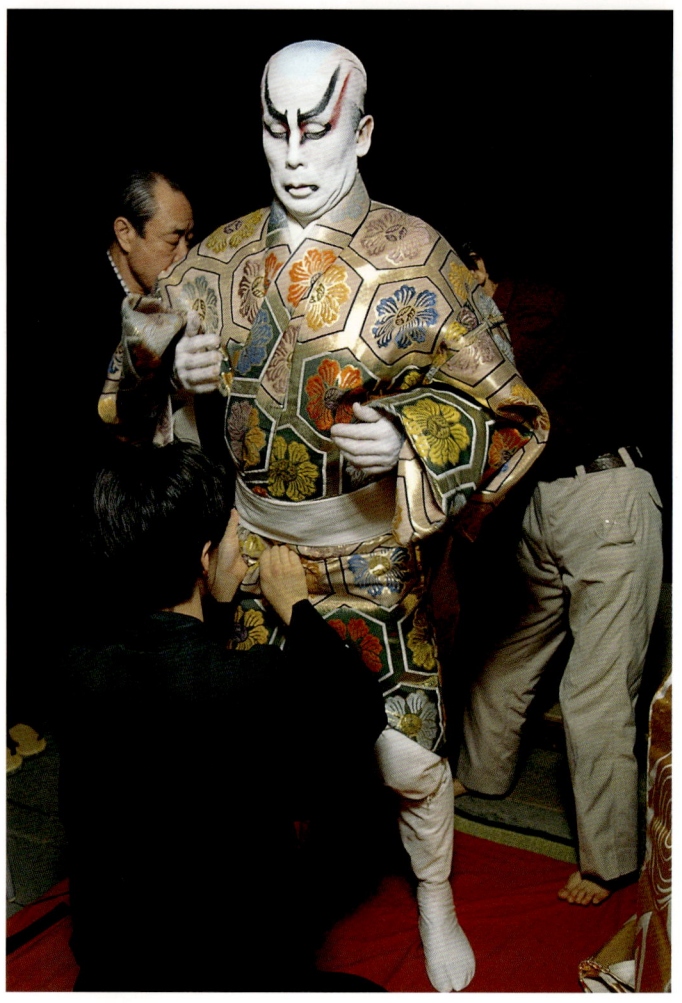

化粧―隈取

歌舞伎の化粧は、役柄と結びついている。二枚目の色男の役の通称を「白塗り」、敵役の意地悪な役人を「赤っ面」などと呼ぶのは、その役割独特の化粧法が、表徴して、役柄そのものの通称となった例である。

歌舞伎では、ごく幼い時は別だが、必ず自身で化粧をする。化粧も、その役者の「芸」の内であり、時には、舞台の上で化粧を変える役すらある。

隈取りは、花道や女形、見得などと共に、いかにも歌舞伎的なイメージを喚起する一種の記号として、一般社会では機能している。しかし実は、隈取りは多種多様な歌舞伎の化粧法の一種であり、ある特定の役に限って用いられるものに過ぎない。(一日中客席に座って見ていても、遂に一人も隈取りをした役が登場しないことも、決して珍しくない。)

たしかに隈取りは、歌舞伎が生んだ、歌舞伎ならではの化粧法である。特に紅で隈を取る「紅隈」は、荒事と結びついて、超人的な力を持った正義の英雄の役を象徴する。『暫』の主人公の「二本隈」はその好例であり、また同じ紅隈でも、助六や曽我五郎に用いられる「剥身」隈は「若衆」の表徴である。『車引』は『菅原伝授手習鑑』という長大な大作の中の、間奏曲風の短い一幕だが、主な人物が皆隈取りをして登場する、隈取り見本市のような趣きがある。

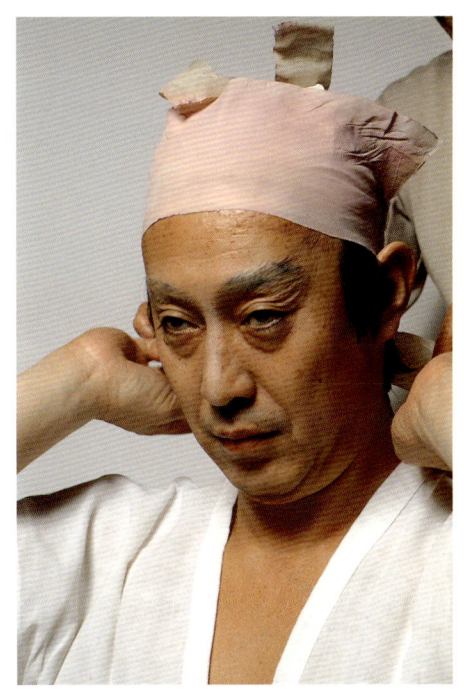

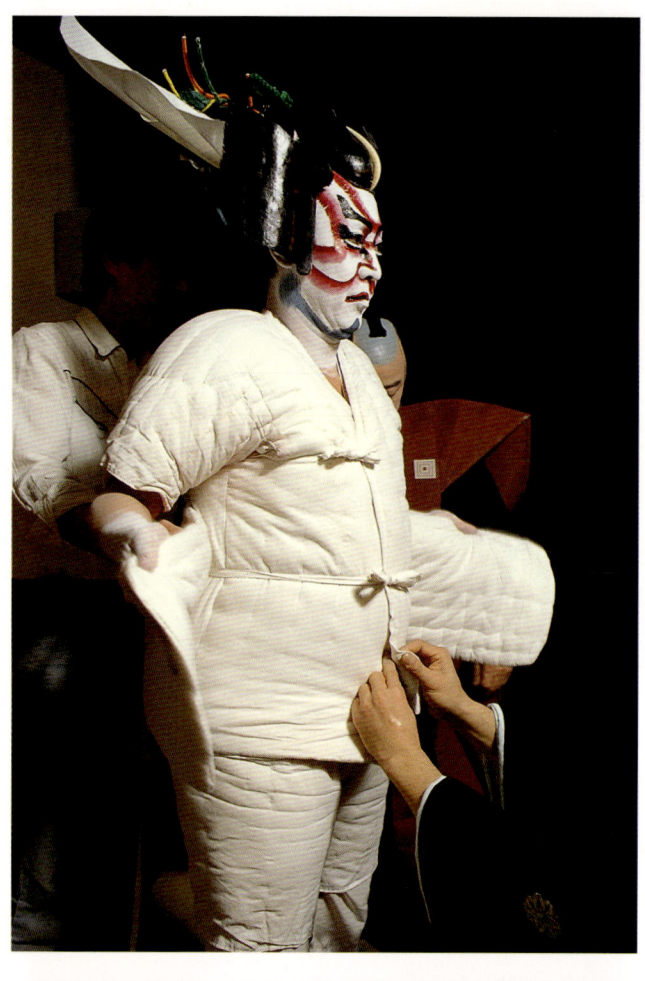

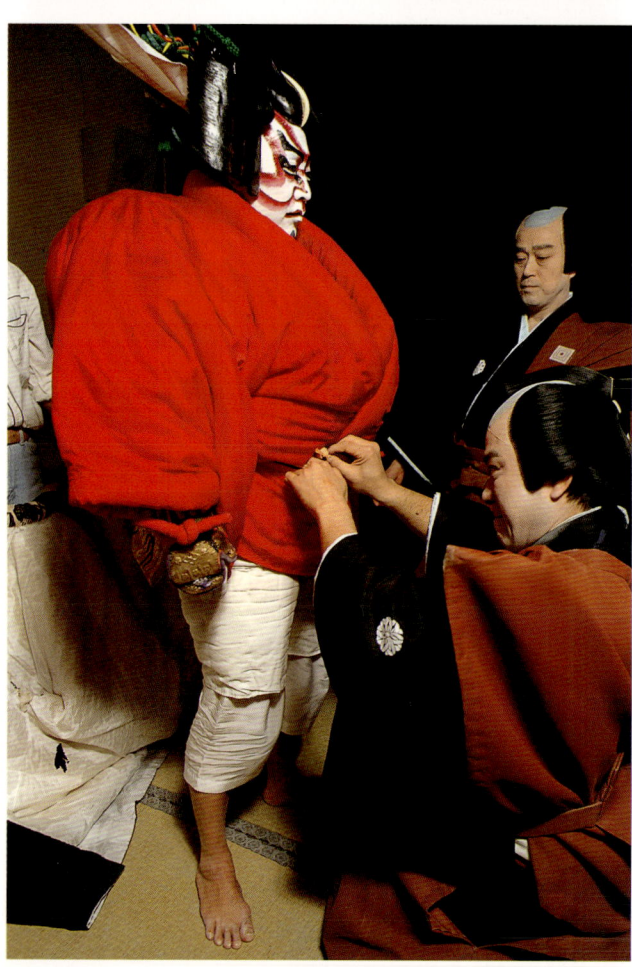

62

暫 Shibaraku

WAIT!

"Shibaraku" is a slightly offbeat title, variously translated as "Wait!" or "Wait a moment!"

The hero of the play, Kamakura Gongorō, appears on stage in the *nihonguma* style of makeup, with enormously exaggerated sideburns known as *kurumabin* and a hairpiece known as a *chikaragami*, of religious origins, wearing an ancient costume consisting of a *suō*, a type of court dress, long trailing *hakama* trousers, sleeves that spread out to evoke the image of a giant bird, and a sword three meters in length. The role of Gongorō is the best example of the righteous *aragoto* super-hero, and the costume reinforces the impression of a gigantic, superhuman being.

The story is simple, a kind of adult fairytale. An evil character of the *kuge-aku*, or "villainous noble" type, wearing blue makeup (*aiguma*) and a wig symbolizing a member of the royal family (*ōji*), plotting to overthrow the emperor, who is wearing a golden crown and white costume, appears accompanied by some rather strange followers, including men with bright red bellies and a "catfish priest" (the play has a slightly comedic touch), and is about to kill a family headed by a weak lord. Just as the good guys are about to be dispatched, the villains are stopped in their tracks by a loud voice shouting, "Wait!" and a "superman" appears from the *hanamichi*....

First staged in 1697. Written by Ichikawa Danjūrō I. *Jidaimono*.

Types of Kabuki Plays

Kabuki has many different faces. In the Meiji period the great scholar Tsubouchi Shōyō likened Kabuki theater to the chimera of Greek legend, because Kabuki has incorporated various other dramatic forms in the course of its development, from elements of its precursors Nō and Kyōgen to the influence of its sister theater Bunraku/*Ningyō jōruri* (doll theater) and the modern theater of the West, and has continued to change throughout its history.

Broadly speaking, Kabuki plays that actually started life as Kabuki are known as *jun* or "pure" Kabuki, while those adapted for the Kabuki stage from doll theater are called *gidayū kyōgen* or *maruhonmono*, and classical Kabuki is composed largely of these two categories. The plays of the *Kabuki Jūhachiban* and works such as those of the two great playwrights Tsuruya Namboku and Kawatake Mokuami form the majority of the "pure" Kabuki repertoire. *Maruhonmono* tend to be majestic works of a serious nature and classical in structure, such as the three most famous plays starting with "Chūshingura." Based as they are on the plays of the doll theater, *maruhonmono* may naturally also be found in the Bunraku repertoire. They are a combination of the Bunraku format in which the *gidayū* (*jōruri*) speaks all the characters' parts and describes the scenes, and the Kabuki format in which the actors are the focus.

In modern times another type of play has emerged: *matsubamemono*, which are Kabuki versions of Nō/Kyōgen, and "new Kabuki," styled on the modern theater of the West.

From a different viewpoint Kabuki plays are often divided into *jidaimono* (historical plays) and *sewamono* (domestic plays). Because Kabuki is fundamentally an art form of the men and women of the Edo era, it creates its own small Kabuki universe from the viewpoint of these people. To them *sewamono* plays were modern theater, drama of the townspeople and farmers, in other words of their own communities. *Jidaimono* were historical pieces, taking for their subject matter events from the upper class world of lords and nobles. This world of aristocratic history and tradition was always viewed through the eyes of the townsman, and strayed into the world of the ordinary citizen of the Tokugawa period as the story unfolded, for example by a prince of the court becoming the lover of a girl from cities like Edo or one of the feudal domains. This is how the romantic, baroque theatrical world of Kabuki, profoundly mystifying in terms of our modern view of historical plays, unfolds on stage.

A study of Kabuki casts will often turn up roles with names like "Tokaiya Gimpei *jitsuwa* Taira no Tomomori" (Tokaiya Gimpei actually Taira no Tomomori). In this particular role, Taira no Tomomori, a well known figure from history (and from the literary classics and legend), disguises himself as a common man (*yatsusu*) by the name of Gimpei, revealing his true identity as the story develops. Thus from beneath the veneer of the *sewa* or domestic world emerges a *jidai* or historical world. As this example from "Yoshitsune Sembonzakura" (Yoshitsune and the Thousand Cherry Trees) demonstrates, this duality of structure is precisely what makes *jidaimono* so fascinating. The difference between *jidaimono* and *sewamono* plays is closely related to the acting styles employed for each. Generally speaking, *jidaimono* plays require acting of a more stylized nature, while *sewamono* performances have greater realism.

狂言の種類

歌舞伎はさまざまな顔を持っている。明治期の碩学坪内逍遥は、歌舞伎をギリシャ神話の怪獣カイミーラにたとえた。先行演劇である能・狂言の要素、姉妹演劇である人形浄瑠璃の影響、さらには西欧の近代劇に至るまで、歌舞伎は生成発展の過程でさまざまな様態を取り込みながら、絶えず流動を続けてきたからである。

大別して、はじめから歌舞伎として作られたものを「純歌舞伎」、人形浄瑠璃として作られた作品を歌舞伎化したものを「義太夫狂言」または「丸本物」と呼び、この両者が古典歌舞伎の大部分を占める。歌舞伎十八番、鶴屋南北・河竹黙阿弥の二大作者の作品などが、純歌舞伎の主なものである。丸本物は『忠臣蔵』などの三大名作をはじめ、古典劇としての骨格を備えた重厚で壮大な作品が多い。本来人形浄瑠璃を本行（原作）とする「丸本物」は、当然ながら文楽のレパートリーと共通する。義太夫（浄瑠璃）がすべての人物の言葉と情景を語る人形劇である文楽の様式と、俳優主体の歌舞伎の様式とを合一して出来あがったジャンルである。

近代になってから、能舞台を模した舞台様式で、能・狂言を歌舞伎化した「松羽目物」や、西欧の近代劇に倣った「新歌舞伎」が作られるようになった。

一方、別な観点から「時代物」と「世話物」に分けることも多い。歌舞伎は基本的に江戸時代の町人芸術なので、町人の観点から歌舞伎という小宇宙は出来あがっている。「世話物」は彼らにとっての現代劇であり、町人・百姓、即ち市民社会のドラマである。「時代物」は、彼らにとっての時代劇であり、同時に大名・公卿など上層社会の世界の出来事を題材とするが、あくまでも町人の観点から見たそれら歴史や伝承の世界の人物たちは、ストーリーの展開と共に徳川時代の市民の世界に紛れ込んで来て、王朝貴族のプリンスが江戸の町娘や在所の村娘と恋人同士になったりする。近代的な歴史劇の常識から見ると摩訶不思議な、ロマン的な、またバロック的な演劇的世界が、こうして繰り広げられるのである。

歌舞伎の配役を見ていると、たとえば「渡海屋銀平実ハ平知盛」といった役名をよく見かける。平知盛という歴史上（または古典や伝説上）の周知の人物が、銀平という庶民に「やつし」て（身を偽って）登場し、物語の展開につれて本体を現わす。それと共に「世話」の世界の表層の下から、「時代」の世界が立ち現われる。『義経千本桜』のこの例のように、その二重構造こそが「時代物」の面白さの真骨頂である。「時代」と「世話」の違いは、演技の様式とも密接に関係する。「時代物」は、概して、様式的にデフォルメされた演技が要求され、一方「世話物」は、よりリアリスティックに演じられる。

仮名手本忠臣蔵
Kanadehon Chūshingura

THE TREASURY OF LOYAL RETAINERS

The affair of the Akō *roshi*, the "forty-seven rōnin," which took place in the Genroku period, the high point of the Tokugawa regime, in the way it captured the public imagination—starting as it did with a dispute between a lord and a high official at Edo castle, and ending with revenge exacted in the city of Edo—was the biggest incident during the two hundred and sixty years of the Edo period. Even had this not been the case, the shogunate prohibited plays dealing directly with the Tokugawa clan or incidents in Edo. Therefore, despite being a dramatization of the most serious incident of the period, "Kanadehon Chūshingura" is set in the Kamakura of the Nambokuchō (Northern and Southern Courts) period.

In the play, the "enemy," Kira Kōzukenosuke, is represented by the regent of the Ashikaga shogun, Kōno Moronō; Asano Takuminokami, who in real life swallowed his bitterness and committed ritual suicide, becomes Enya Hangan, who flees to the court of the south, burning with hatred, and meets his end after Moronō takes his wife; and the leader of the vendetta, Ōishi Kuranosuke, becomes the very similarly titled Ōboshi Yuranosuke, whose surname means "great star." The audience is able to match this incident involving characters from the world of the *Taiheiki* with the incident that actually occurred in Edo and to enjoy a dual structure of truth and illusion.

The wounding of Kira that actually took place in the *matsu no rōka* (passageway) of Edo castle was the result of a dispute between Kira and Asano on the occasion of a reception for imperial envoys from Kyoto, but in the play it arises from a fight between Moronō and Momonoi Wakasanosuke at Kamakura Tsurugaoka Hachiman Shrine, over the helmet of Nitta Yoshisada, a vanquished enemy of the shogun, ending in an ironic twist in which Enya Hangan, the *aiyaku*, or "colleague," of Wakanosuke wounds Moronō in the *matsu no ma* (Pine Tree Chamber) at the Ashikaga mansion.

In the usual manner of the *maruhon jidaimono* "history," in other words, an incident taking place in the upper echelons of society encroaches on the "*sewa*" world of the townspeople and farmers, and the drama reaches its climax. The tragedy of the love of Hayano Kanpei, retainer of Enya Hangan, and Okaru, lady's maid of Enya's wife Lady Kaoyo, has been the most popular scene in the Kabuki version of "Chūshingura" since the play's early days. Kanpei, failing to complete an important task as a result of his love for Okaru, hurries to join his fellow avengers and in the process commits a series of irreversible blunders.

The authors also depict the tragedy of the family of a samurai that restrained Enya Hangan, resulting in the attack on Moronō that only wounded and did not kill him. A dispute between two great lords inviting a series of tragedies for their retainers and families—this is the theme running through the epic "Kanadehon Chūshingura," which is performed over an entire day (and in fact is still only around two-thirds of the whole play). "Chūshingura" is by no means simply a bloody tale of revenge.

First staged as Kabuki in 1748. Adapted from *Ningyō jōruri* by Takeda Izumo II, Namiki Senryū, and Miyoshi Shōraku. *Maruhon jidaimono.*

73

菅原伝授手習鑑

Sugawara Denju Tenarai Kagami

Sugawara's Secrets of Calligraphy

Together with "Chūshingura" and "Sembonzakura," this is counted as one of the three great Kabuki masterpieces, many say the greatest. All the main scenes—"Dōmyōji Temple," the mysterious story of a sacred dynasty; "Kuruma-biki" (the struggle for the carriage), the ultimate beauty of form in a soul-stirring interlude; "Ga no Iwai" (Sata Village), depicting the misery of the cowherd youth who died young; and "Terakoya," full of mystery and suspense—when viewed from start to finish unfold in a superb manner, and when viewed independently constitute complete acts in themselves.

The three authors are said to have contrived a plot in which the parting of a parent and child is depicted in three separate scenes, but this works perfectly in accordance with the dramatic concept of the *maruhon jidaimono*, in which a dispute "above the clouds" (in the palace), splits the household of an innocent commoner, (*toneri*, the cowherd), setting the three brothers against each other.

"Dōmyōji Temple" depicts the parting of the main character, Sugawara no Michizane, also known as Kan Shōjō, and his daughter Princess Kariya. Shōjō is falsely charged with conniving in the love between the princess and Prince Tokiyo by the rebel and enemy of the state, Fujiwara Shihei, who is plotting to overthrow the emperor, and is exiled to the outlying region of Tsukushi (Kyushu). The part of Kan Shōjō, a man of unimpeachable moral fortitude, is the most prestigious of all roles in Kabuki, and a difficult part that demands dignity and a high level of artistic skill from the actor who plays it.

"Kuruma-biki" is a soul-stirring interlude between two epic tragedies. The triplet brothers Umeōmaru, Matsuōmaru, and Sakuramaru are driven apart by the conflict between Kan Shōjō, Shihei, and Prince Tokiyo, their respective masters. The three brothers and the villainous noble Shihei all wear attractive makeup.

In "Ga no Iwai," Sakuramaru—who has acted as go-between in the love of Prince Tokiyo and Princess Kariya—feels he is to blame for all that has happened and kills himself, on the very day that the three brothers are gathered with their spouses for the seventieth birthday of their father Shirotayū.

In "Terakoya," a retainer of Kan Shōjō by the name of Takebe Genzō—who although disinherited for a forbidden love has been trusted with the secrets of calligraphy—and his wife Tonami are secretly hiding the young lord Kan Shūsai. Shihei, however, eventually realizes this and sends a messenger ordering Genzō to present the head of Shūsai. Who else should be sent to inspect the head but Matsuōmaru? Genzō is at a loss. Unexpectedly Matsuōmaru sacrifices his own child to repay the kindness of Kan Shōjō. This kind of unexpected reversal, in which a seemingly villainous character turns out to be one of the "good guys," is known in Kabuki as *modori*.

First staged in 1746 as Kabuki. Adapted from *Ningyō jōruri* by Takeda Izumo I & II, Namiki Senryū, and Miyoshi Shōraku. *Maruhon jidaimono*.

80

Yoshitsune and the Thousand Cherry Trees

Like "Kanjinchō" this is a story of Minamoto no Yoshitsune, following his destruction of the Heike and exile from the capital at the hands of his brother Yoritomo, and his subsequent journey. While at a glance Yoshitsune would appear to have the leading role, he is more of a common thread holding the play together, the lead roles in the three main scenes of the play being at various times the valiant generals of the Heike, who are supposed to lie in a watery grave off the west coast of Japan, the sushi shop family who cannot forget their obligation to the Heike, and a fox who takes the form of Yoshitsune's loyal retainer Satō Tadanobu and protects Yoshitsune's beloved mistress Shizuka Gozen.

The war between the Minamoto and Taira clans (Genji and Heike) is both historical fact and the subject of the epic poetry classic "Heike Monogatari" (The Tale of the Heike), for centuries the episode in their own history with which Japanese have been most familiar. The unfortunate young noble, Yoshitsune, has been the character people love and empathize with most, and his life has been the theme of many stories passed down over the years. In this play Yoshitsune has left the stage of history and gone into exile, and the three Heike generals Tomomori, Koremori and Noritsune, who in fact died, have survived and are living a different "truth" to "the truth of history." A different truth to the truth of history—the story Kabuki always endeavors to tell, and in no play is this so apparent as in "Yoshitsune Sembonzakura."

In the scene "Tokaiya/Daimotsu no ura" (The House of the Boatman/The Beach at Daimotsu Bay), the valiant Heike general Taira no Tomomori—who in fact met his demise in the naval battle at Dannoura—has disguised himself as the boatman Tokaiya Gimpei, pretending that the child emperor is his own child, and is waiting for a chance to rise up against the Minamoto. Who, then, should come along to hire his boat but the exiled Yoshitsune! Tomomori challenges Yoshitsune once again to a battle at sea, but the fortunes of war are against him and he is defeated.

Entrusting the child-emperor to the care of Yoshitsune, he ties an anchor to his body and commits suicide by leaping into the sea.

"The Sushi Shop" is a tragedy involving commoners, as is the rule in the third act of a *jōruri* narrative play. Yazaemon, who is indebted to the Heike, hides the Heike general Taira no Koremori, but his daughter Osato falls in love with the general, not realizing his true identity. Meanwhile Yazaemon's delinquent son Gonta does guess the stranger's identity and informs on him to the Genji authorities. In despair, Yazaemon stabs his corrupt son, mortally wounding him. In an ironic twist, Gonta had in fact planned to sacrifice himself to protect Koremori and his family. Here also we may observe the Kabuki convention of *modori*.

From "Yoshino-yama" ("Michiyuki") to "Shinokiri" (The Mansion of Kawatsura Hōgen), we see the loyal retainer Satō Tadanobu protecting Shizuka Gozen, who pines for her lover Yoshitsune. In actual fact it is not Tadanobu but a fox that has taken on the form of Tadanobu. The skin on the drum known as Hatsune which was given to Shizuka by Yoshitsune as a memento, is in fact the hide of the fox's parents. The filial devotion of the fox strikes a chord with Yoshitsune, always fighting his own flesh and blood and now exiled because of his brother.

First staged as Kabuki in 1748. Adapted from *Ningyō jōruri* by Takeda Izumo II, Namiki Senryū, and Miyoshi Shōraku. *Maruhon jidaimono.*

義経千本桜 Yoshitsune Sembonzakura

妹背山婦女庭訓
Imoseyama Onna Teikin

EXEMPLARY TALES FOR WOMEN

Set in the seventh century at the ancient court, this is the most romantic work in Kabuki and the most magnificent in scale. In the past, one critic likened it to the operas of Wagner with their backdrop of ancient Germanic legend.

Soga no Iruka is a historical figure from an old noble family who did actually live in the seventh century; however, in this play he seizes the throne in a coup, banishing the blind emperor Tenji. Iruka is the greatest villain among all villains on the Kabuki stage, and appears in the ghostly superhuman form of a villainous noble, his face painted white and blue.

In "Yoshinogawa," Daihanji Kiyosumi and Sadaka, widow of the Dazai clan, who face each other across a river and are now both unwillingly under the authority of Iruka, cooperate to enable the love of their children Koganosuke and Hinadori to reach fruition, while maintaining their traditional rivalry. As a result of the increasing power of Iruka, this consideration for each other ends with the two young people taking their own lives. Watching the pair of lovers from rival families one is reminded of Romeo and Juliet.

The heroine of the scenes from "Michiyuki" to "Mikasa-yama Goten" (The Palace) is the pitiful young country girl Omiwa, who burns with passion having fallen in love with the young noble Fujiwara no Tankai, who has disguised himself as the hat seller Motome and intends to bring down Iruka. Omiwa is unaware of the true rank of the young man. Following a fight over Tankai (Motome) with Princess Tachibana, Iruka's younger sister, she follows the pair into Iruka's palace. As part of his scheme Motome (Tankai) exchanges marriage vows with the sister of his enemy. Unaware that it is all a ruse, Omiwa is inflamed with jealousy. The blood of a pure maiden driven mad by jealousy—this was the secret potion needed to destroy the apparition Iruka.

Omiwa is a poor young girl wandering into a bewitched palace, like Alice lost in the world through the looking-glass.

First staged as Kabuki in 1771. Adapted from *Ningyō jōruri* by Chikamatsu Hanji and others. *Maruhon jidaimono*.

Ichinotani Futaba Gunki 一谷嫩軍記

CHRONICLE OF THE BATTLE OF ICHINOTANI
—*Kumagai's Camp*

This is another tragedy based on an episode in "The Tale of the Heike," the epic poem of the conflict between the Minamoto (Genji) and Taira (Heike) clans, and sheds light on another truth hidden in the gray area between history and fiction.

Taira no Atsumori, a young nobleman of the Heike defeated by the Genji at the battle of Ichinotani, is actually the son of the previous emperor, and Minamoto no Yoshitsune, overall commander of the Genji forces, gives his general Kumagai Naozane a secret order. Kumagai steals Atsumori away from the battlefield and hides him. Ordered to kill Atsumori in order to obey his master, Kumagai is forced to turn his hand against his own son of the same age, Kojirō Naoie, who is taking part in his first battle. The callous reasoning behind this is protection of the imperial line, which supercedes the conflict between Heike and Genji. Furthermore, to Naozane and his wife Sagami, Atsumori's mother Fuji-no-kata is the woman who saved their lives sixteen years previously, in their younger days, when they had broken the rules of the palace where they were both employed and had formed a relationship, which resulted in Sagami becoming pregnant with Kojirō. To obey the order he cannot avoid, Kumagai hardens his heart and kills his son. Disillusioned with humanity he then leaves the battle field to become a priest.

First staged as Kabuki in 1752. Adapted from *Ningyō jōruri* by Namiki Sōsuke and others. *Maruhon jidaimono*.

THE STORY OF LORD ICHIJŌ ŌKURA

鬼一法眼三略巻
Kiichi Hōgen Sanryaku no Maki

一條大蔵譚
Ichijō Ōkura Monogatari

The conflict between the Genji and the Heike also forms the backdrop to this play, but here Yoshitsune is still a boy, and the era is that of despotic rule by the Heike.

Ichijō Ōkura-kyo Naganari is a noble of the court but a secret Genji sympathizer. With the whole country suffering under the tyrannical yoke of the Heike, revealing his true loyalties would mean risking his life. The method Ōkura-kyo adopts to protect his freedom of thought is to deceive the world by playing the fool, abandoning himself to make-believe and hiding his genius, like Hamlet. Nobody realizes his true identity as a wise young noble; all take him for a born fool. Taira no Kiyomori, leader of the Heike, having killed the head of the Genji clan Minamoto no Yoshitomo and taken his wife Tokiwa, hands her on to Ōkura-kyo. Ōkura-kyo continues to act the fool, and his wife Tokiwa abandons herself to archery.

Genji retainer Yoshioka Kijirō and his wife infiltrate the palace to gauge Tokiwa's true feelings and find her shooting arrows into a portrait of Kiyomori on the pretext of archery practice. She is discovered by the villainous chief retainer. In one dangerous moment there is the flash of a *naginata* sword, the villainous retainer is slain, and Ōkura-kyo appears....

First staged as Kabuki in 1732. Adapted from *Ningyō jōruri* by Bunkōdō and Hasegawa Senshi. *Maruhon jidai-mono.*

Honchō Nijūshi Kō 本朝廿四孝

TWENTY-FOUR DUTIFUL SONS

Set in the Sengoku (Warring States) period. Princess Yaegaki, daughter of Nagao Kenshin, lord of Echigo (Niigata) and Shinshu (Nagano), is a young woman brought up in seclusion and in love with the idea of love, who spends her days staring at a portrait of Takeda Katsuyori, a man with whom for political reasons her father has arranged a marriage, but whom she has yet to actually meet. Hearing a rumor that Katsuyori has died, she burns incense in front of his portrait and mourns for the fiancé who left this world before they could even meet.

When she stops to listen to a voice in the next room, who should it be but Katsuyori! She rushes next door and clings to him, but the man insists he is not Katsuyori. The princess is ashamed of her immodest behavior, but still feels instinctively that this man is her fiancé. She asks Nureginu, a maid servant traveling with the man, who intimates that the man is indeed Katsuyori. Nureginu extracts a terrible price for revealing the secret. She tells the princess to steal the helmet of Suwa Hosshō, which is hidden in the inner garden, without her father Kenshin finding out. If Yaegaki chooses her love for Katsuyori she betrays her father. Princesses in love are blind to all else....

First staged as Kabuki in 1766. Adapted from *Ningyō jōruri* by Chikamatsu Hanji and others. *Maruhon jidaimono.*

源平布引滝 Gempei Nunobiki no Taki
実盛物語 Sanemori Monogatari

THE NUNOBIKI WATERFALL
—The Recitation of Sanemori

The Heike are at the height of their power, and Saitō Sanemori—a Heike warrior originally with connections also to the Genji—and his comrade Senō Jurō visit the home of fisherman Kurosuke on the shore of Lake Biwa, where the wife of Genji general Kiso Yoshikata is hiding. The pregnant wife is about to give birth, and if the child is a boy the pair have been given strict orders to cut out the Genji roots there and then by killing him. Sanemori in his white makeup and *namajime* wig is the sensible man of the world, a man of both reason and sentiment, while hateful Senō, with his bright red face and white hair, has the red visage of the vicious official. Senō himself, however, has an unexpected secret.

Having finally worked through this difficult problem, Sanemori relates to Tarokichi, grandson of Kurosuke, his prediction of what will happen in twenty years' time. When the child born today becomes the general Kiso Yoshinaka and fights the Heike, he foretells, I, who by that time will be an old fighter, will be killed by you who will have grown up to become a young warrior. This is an excellent work that emerged from the actual story of the famous white-haired warrior Saitō Sanemori of the "Heike Monogatari."

First staged as Kabuki in 1757. Adapted from *Ningyō jōruri* by Namiki Senryū and Miyoshi Shōraku. *Maruhon jidaimono.*

Love Letters from the Licensed Quarters

Izaemon, young master of the merchant family of Fujiya, becomes lover and soulmate of Yūgiri, a courtesan of Shinmachi in Osaka, and is left destitute following his disinheritance for squandering large sums on his nocturnal activities.

On a day when all are busy preparing for the New Year's festivities, Izaemon, reduced to wearing a paper kimono, stands shivering in the cold wind outside the Yoshidaya Kizaemon teahouse he once frequented every night. The owners of the Yoshidaya, remembering their former regular, give the pathetic Izaemon a warm welcome and allow him to see Yūgiri. While Yūgiri entertains another client Izaemon waits, alternating between joy and shame, nostalgia and conceit, and venting his anger at Yūgiri for taking so long to show up even though he desperately wants to see her.

The various phases of a man in love are expressed in different ways in the *wagoto* ("gentle") style of acting used for romantic male parts. No one could possibly dislike Izaemon, a playboy with the heart of an innocent. The *kamiko* ("paper kimono") worn by Izaemon is a symbol of *wagoto* and is a distinctive elegant purple.

First staged as Kabuki in 1808. Adapted from Yūgiri Awa no Naruto by Chikamatsu Monzaemon. *Sewamono*.

Kuruwa Bunshō 廓文章

青砥稿花紅彩画
弁天娘女男白浪
Aoto Zōshi Hana no Nishiki-e
Benten Musume Meo no Shiranami

THE GLORIOUS PICTURE BOOK OF AOTO'S EXPLOITS; AND ALSO MISS BENTEN THE MALE / FEMALE BANDIT

Benten Kozō Kikunosuke is a young rogue who strayed from home as a boy and joined a gang of thieves. Possessed of all the feminine charms of a woman, he takes his alias from the goddess Benten, and disguises himself in the long sleeved *furisode* kimono of a young lady of good breeding to do his wicked work. On this particular day he teams up with an older thief, Nangō Rikimaru, and once again pretends to be the daughter of a high-ranking warrior family, visiting the Hamamatsuya kimono store to buy her wedding trousseau. There he appears to steal something, but in actual fact has deliberately used a sample bought from another shop as part of the ruse. The shop assistants panic when they think he has been shoplifting and attack him, wounding him on the forehead.

The thief Benten Kozō, who up until that moment had been a young lady, suddenly throws off his disguise to reveal a cherry tattoo over the upper half of his body. The young lady customer turns out to have been a male thief.

As these events unfold an impressive warrior by the name of Nippon Daemon steps in to mediate. He is an imposter as well, being in fact the leader of the gang (the others are Akaboshi Jūzaburō and Tadanobu Rihei, and together they are known as the Shiranami Gonin Otoko, literally "the five thieves.") The play is a surreal daydream set in a degenerate *ancien régime* with a satisfying touch of the picaresque.

First staged in 1862. Written by Kawatake Mokuami. *Sewamono*.

籠釣瓶花街酔醒
Kagotsurube Sato no Eizame

KAGOTSURUBE THE BEWITCHING SWORD

Wealthy country bumpkin Jirozaemon arrives in Edo for some sightseeing with his manservant Jiroku, and is mesmerized by the courtesan Yatsuhashi, then at the peak of her allure. Jirozaemon is a rich man, but cursed with an ugly pockmarked visage, and is a bundle of insecurities. While telling himself there is no way this woman can ever be his alone, he begins visiting her frequently. For her part, while she may be at the height of her popularity, Yatsuhashi is still a courtesan, so accepts his custom. Jirozaemon is in ecstasy. He offers to buy her freedom if she will be his wife. The woman already has a lover, and is bound by complex circumstances. Recklessly she humiliates the brash and conceited Jirozaemon by saying no to his offer in public. He meekly takes his leave, but reappears three months later and kills Yatsuhashi with the bewitching sword Kagotsurube he has brought from his home in the country.

First staged in 1888. Written by Kawatake Shinshichi III. *Sewamono*.

東海道四谷怪談 Tōkaidō Yotsuya Kaidan

YOTSUYA GHOST STORIES

Tamiya Iemon, husband of Oiwa, watches sardonically from the sidelines as his comrades plot revenge for the humiliation of their master.

However, not only is he living the easy life, but when the granddaughter of a high-ranking enemy falls in love with him he abandons Oiwa and his newborn child and consents to marry the girl and become part of her family. Iemon is an irresponsible and amoral character. Not only has he just killed Oiwa's father following the man's discovery of another of his evil deeds, but he is now feigning innocence and making Oiwa feel obliged to him by saying he will avenge the death.

Oiwa, daughter of a serious-minded warrior, never questions this husband for a moment but endures their poverty and even secretly prostitutes herself to help her man, who has no income. Eventually she realizes Iemon has betrayed her in many ways. Tricked into drinking poison that changes her appearance, her hair falls out and her face is transformed into a horrible festering mess before she dies and becomes a ghost, cursing Iemon.

First staged in 1825. Written by Tsuruya Namboku IV. *Sewamono*.

115

SCARRED YOSABURŌ

与話情浮名横櫛　Yowa Nasake Ukina no Yokogushi

Young rake Yosaburō, steeped in debauchery and disowned by his parents, is in Kisarazu on the other side of the narrow Edo Bay, where he has been sent to behave himself, when he encounters Otomi, mistress of the local gangster boss. They form an intimate bond as fellow Edoites reminiscing about their home town. The gangster discovers their relationship and cuts Yosaburō in thirty-four places all over his body before throwing him into the sea. Otomi throws herself into the sea also but is rescued.

Three years pass. Yosaburō has become an outlaw by the name of Kirare Yosa (literally, "Yosa who is cut") and sets out at the direction of his cohort Kōmori Yasu, who has a tattoo of a bat on his cheek, to the home of the mistress of the head clerk of a wealthy merchant to extort money. Who should be there but Otomi, whom he assumed to be dead. This is all your doing, he accuses her, and look what I've become. Yosaburō fails to notice his own self-centeredness. This tale of a corrupted connection between a man and a woman in the mature metropolis of Edo is a play for adults.

First staged in 1853. Written by Segawa Jokō III. *Sewamono*.

NAOZAMURAI AND MICHITOSE

Kataoka Naojirō was once a warrior, but has gone down in the world and is now an outlaw. His alias "Nao-zamurai" hints at his past status. He is the lover of the courtesan Michitose, but orders are out for his arrest as the perpetrator of several crimes in Edo, so this night he must flee far away.

An evening just before the onset of spring. Large falls of snow are rare in Edo at this time of the year. Nao-zamurai has reached Iriya on the outskirts of Edo, and on a whim enters a soba (noodle) shop. There he hears a rumor that Michitose is close by, recovering from an illness, and goes to see her and say goodbye. The poignant rendition of a *kiyomoto* tune from the house next door transforms the parting of the wretched good-for-nothing and the low-class courtesan into an enchanted dream. It becomes the love story of a sophisticated man and woman of Edo. Finally his pursuers turn up, and Nao-zamurai runs away, crying in grief that he will never meet Michitose again in this world.

First staged in 1881. Written by Kawatake Mokuami. *Sewamono*.

Kumo ni Magou Ueno no Hatsuhana
天衣紛上野初花

Yuki no Yūbe Iriya no Azemichi
雪暮夜入谷畦道

119

桜姫東文章
Sakura-hime Azuma Bunshō

THE SCARLET PRINCESS AND HER STORY IN THE EAST

No other princess in Kabuki experiences the vicissitudes of fortune like Princess Sakura. This noble princess, following a single savage encounter in the darkness, runs away in pursuit of her ravisher, the rogue Tsurigane Gonsuke. They marry, but in order to learn the foul language of the gutter Sakura becomes a prostitute in the lowest order of brothel. (The opposite of the "My Fair Lady" scenario in which the flower seller heroine learns from Professor Higgins how to speak in a refined manner and is transformed into a lady.) But there's more… In a previous life the princess was a young page by the name of Shiragikumaru at a Buddhist temple, who committed suicide with Seigen, a priest in training. Seigen survived and, full of remorse for this mistake, eventually became the high priest at Kiyomizudera. Discovering that Princess Sakura is the reincarnation of Shiragikumaru, to compensate for his survival he does everything he can to be with her, even breaking his vows. The princess, who lets her passions guide her, abandons Seigen in pursuit of Gonsuke. A bizarre and sensuous romance.

First staged in 1817. Written by Tsuruya Nanboku IV. *Sewamono*.

Tachiyaku: Male Roles

Tachiyaku is a general term for male roles apart from those of the *onnagata*. The *nimaime*, or "second," for example, is the handsome lover, while the *sanmaime*, or "third," is the clown, with these terms referring originally to the ranking of the roles played by the actors.

The terms *aragoto*, *wagoto*, and *jitsugoto* on the other hand refer to styles of acting used for different characters. The *aragoto* acting technique involves distortion of the characteristics of righteousness and strength by exaggeration/magnification. Righteous superheroes like the lead in "Shibaraku" represent *aragoto* in its purest form; however, when *aragoto* is used for a *wakashugata*, or youngster, the role becomes a *mukimi* role like that of Soga no Gorō, and, if a touch of *wagoto* is added, a dandy like Sukeroku—a strong and just man with the added feature of an elegant erotic appeal.

Wagoto roles complement those of the *onnagata* courtesan, and combine the sophistication of the ladies' man flirting with courtesans in the erotic and playful surroundings of the pleasure quarters with the fragility of a man who abandons all for love, and occasional touches of slovenliness and humor. In terms of roles this is the *nimaime*, or lover, but not all *nimaime* roles are in the *wagoto* style. A dashing type of *nimaime* warrior known as a *sabakiyaku*, who appears in *jidaimono* (historical plays) and resolves disputes perfectly through a combination of reason and emotion, is also known as a *namajime* from the type of wig he wears.

The *jitsugoto* style, while used for righteous characters in the same manner as *aragoto*, does not employ exaggerated expressions of strength, but represents a dependable, sober man in the prime of life, courageous and intelligent in a more realistic manner. No matter how strong he might be, no one would want an *aragoto* hero for a leader. The greatest leader in Kabuki, Ōboshi Yuranosuke of "Chūshingura," is a typical example of a *jitsugoto* hero, while Benkei of "Kanjinchō" is probably the ideal hero, a scholar/warrior combination of the valor and childlike simplicity of the *aragoto* and the cool control of the *jitsugoto*.

Katakiyaku, or "foes," come in many forms. They may represent evil on a massive scale, wearing *aiguma*, or blue makeup, as opposed to the *aragoto* hero in his *beniguma*, or red makeup—for example as superhuman villains like the *kugeaku*, or "villainous nobles," plotting to usurp the power of the emperor, or the villains who plot to bring down the state, *kunikuzushi*—or they may be minor crooks, at the other end of the scale, known as *hagataki*. There are also female villains. The allure of evil is just one facet of the allure of Kabuki and is the domain of the *tachiyaku*.

「立役」とは、女形に対して、男性の役を総称する用語である。たとえば「二枚目」とは色男の役であり「三枚目」とは道化役だが、こういう言葉は、元々、俳優の地位と役柄を現わす用語に由来している。

一方「荒事」「和事」「実事」という言い方は、役柄を表現する演技の仕方を指す言葉である。「荒事」とは、正義と力を誇張・拡大というデフォルメを通じて表現する演技法のことである。『暫』の主人公のような正義のスーパーマンが最も本来的な意味での荒事だが、それが「若衆方」という二枚目の未成年と結びつくと、曽我五郎のような剥身隈を取る役になり、さらに和事味を加えると助六のような、正義と力の上に優雅な色気を加えたダンディになる。

「和事」とは、女形の「傾城」に対応する。廓という色と遊びの場で遊女と戯れる色男の優美さの上に、恋にうつつを抜かす男の弱さや時にはだらしなさ、滑稽さまで掛け合わせたものをいう。役柄でいえば「二枚目」だが、すべての二枚目が和事なわけではない。「捌き役」といって、情理兼ね備えた、争いごとを見事に捌いて見せる「時代物」に登場する颯爽たる二枚目の武士の役は、この種の役がつける鬘の種類から「生締」役とも呼ばれる。

「実事」とは、同じ正義でも荒事のような誇張した力の表現ではなく、もっと現実に即した智力と胆力を備えた、渋みのある頼もしい壮年の男性の表徴である。どんなに強くても、われわれは荒事のヒーローを統率者に持とうとは思わないだろう。歌舞伎に登場する最もすぐれた統率者『忠臣蔵』の大星由良之助は実事の代表であり、『勧進帳』の弁慶は、荒事の豪勇と稚気と、実事の沈着冷静を兼備した、文武両道の理想的な英雄といえる。

「敵役」には、紅隈を取る荒事に対する、藍隈を取る「公卿悪」という国家簒奪の超人的な悪や、一国を略奪する「国崩し」というスケールの大きい悪から、「端敵」という悪の手先の小悪、さらには女の敵役までさまざまな役柄がある。悪の魅力も歌舞伎の魅力のひとつであり、これも立役の勤める領分である。

129

Onnagata: Female Roles

The rivulet that had its source in the *Kabuki odori* of Izumo no Okuni in 1603 eventually changed course dramatically as the Tokugawa Shogunate successively outlawed women's Kabuki and *wakashu Kabuki*—which relied on the charms of young boys to attract audiences. This rivulet became deeper and wider to form the powerful current of Kabuki that continues to flow in the present day. These changes took place over a period of around half a century from the origins of Kabuki as established by Okuni.

They also encouraged the emergence of the genuine *onnagata*; that is, the beginnings of the art of the *onnagata*, in which female characters are played not by young women or boys, but an art form in which males play women's roles most beautifully and intensely, both in appearance (externally) and feelings (internally). The skill and spirit this requires form the "art" of the *onnagata*.

Yoshizawa Ayame I, the first and greatest *onnagata* in history, said that the roots of *onnagata* acting lie in the role of the *keisei*, or courtesan. Women like Agemaki and Yūgiri are the most elevated type of courtesan, representing the feminine ideal of a woman who gently provides a refuge for her man from the outside world. Yatsuhashi, while belonging to the same group of high-class prostitutes, gives a more realistic portrayal of the misery and the vicious nature of life in the world known as the pleasure quarters.

The *hime*, or princess, is a young lady raised in seclusion, which means that once she falls in love, she throws herself into that love body and soul. A woman's heart, willing to do anything for love—this is the essence of the *hime*. Particularly important *hime* roles are Yaegaki-hime of "Honchō Nijūshi Kō," Toki-hime of "Kamakura Sandaiki," and Yuki-hime of "Kinkakuji" (Gion Sairei Shinkōki). These three are often called the *sanhime*, the "three princesses."

Among *musume*, or young girls, there are the *machi musume* of the city and the girls of the country. Like the *hime*, these girls lose themselves in love. Unlike the *hime*, however, they live in the towns and villages and are thus more familiar to the general audience.

The *nyōbō*, or married woman, is a metaphor for the essential nature of woman as wife or mother. *Nyōbō* come in many guises, from the high-ranking mistresses of warrior families to the wives of townsmen or farmers, and as the everyday expression *sewa nyōbō* (devoted wife) indicates, the nature of the *nyōbō* is to dedicate her life to her husband and children.

The *katahazushi* is a high-ranking lady-in-waiting employed in the home of a lord, and the expression refers to the type of wig worn in this role. The costumes of Kabuki (clothing, wigs, makeup) impart to each role a physical form; therefore such terms are frequently used for particular types of character. Princesses in love generally wear a long-sleeved kimono of scarlet patterned satin, so are often called *akahime*, or "red princesses."

There are no enemy roles for *onnagata*, because the role of the *onnagata* is to express the beauty of the feminine heart. Female villains are played by the *tachiyaku*.

女形

　1603年、出雲の阿国の「かぶき踊り」を水源とする流れは、やがて「女かぶき」と少年たちの美しさが売物の「若衆かぶき」が、徳川幕府によって相次いで禁止された時点で、大きく流れを変え、川幅も深さも増して、今日までつながる「歌舞伎」という大河になった。阿国かぶき発祥から約半世紀余のことである。
　それはまた、取りも直さず、本格的な「女形」の誕生を促す契機でもあった。若い女性や少年の容姿ではなく、成人男子が女の役を演じる「芸」によって勝負する女形芸が、ここに始まる。女の容姿（外観）と心（内面）とをいかに美しく、深く演じて見せるか。そのための技術と精神。併せてそれが「芸」である。
　女形史上最初にして最大の名女形だった芳沢あやめは、「傾城」即ち遊女の役に女形芸の根本があると言った。揚巻や夕霧は、やさしく男を包んでくれる女性の理想像としての、最高級の遊女である。八ツ橋は、同じ高級な遊女でも、もっとリアルに、廓という世界に生きる女の哀しさやしたたかさを見せる。
　「姫」は深窓に育った令嬢で、それだけに、ひとたび恋をしたら一筋に突き進む。恋のためには何ものをも顧みない女心。それが姫という存在の本質である。姫の中で特に重要な役として、『本朝廿四孝』の八重垣姫、『鎌倉三代記』の時姫、『金閣寺』の雪姫を、よく「三姫」という。
　「娘」には都会の「町娘」と田舎の娘とがある。彼女たちも、姫と同じく、恋のために燃える。ただ、一般の観客にもっと身近な、町や村に住む少女であるところが違う。
　ミセスを意味する「女房」は、「妻」もしくは「母」としての女性の本性を形容として捕らえた役柄である。高い身分の武家の女房から、町人百姓の女房までさまざまあるが、「世話女房」という言葉が一般用語として広まったように、夫とわが子のために生きるのが女房の本質である。
　「片はずし」という役柄は、御殿勤めをする高級な奥女中だが、この用語は、この役柄の鬘の種類から来ている。歌舞伎の扮装（衣裳・鬘・化粧）は役柄の形象化だから、その用語が、しばしば役柄の代名詞になる。恋に燃える姫は、大概緋綸子の振袖を着るので、「赤姫」とよく呼ばれる。
　女形には敵役はない。女形は、女心の美しさを表現するのが本分だからである。女の悪人＝敵役は、立役の俳優が演じる。

Leading *Onnagata* of Modern Times: Utaemon and Tamasaburō

If we were to nominate the two leading *onnagata* of the half-century or so of Kabuki history since World War II, the names that come to mind would have to be Nakamura Utaemon (Utaemon VI) and Bando Tamasaburō (Tamasaburō V). If by great *onnagata* we mean famous actors who have been *onnagata*, any number of actors could qualify, but if we mean those *onnagata* who have both reflected the times and held their own against the times to create their own unique aesthetic, then these two cannot be omitted.

Utaemon rose to prominence in the change of generations after the war, as one of the so-called Big Six that sustained Kabuki in the postwar period and were feted by audiences along with Onoe Baikō (Baikō VII), another great *onnagata* of the same generation. Among these prominent actors it was Utaemon who most vividly brought to life his own kind of beauty on stage and mesmerized audiences, all the while struggling with difficult circumstances in an era of major change in the values and aesthetics of society. Beneath a slight and fragile, old-fashioned exterior, this "man," who looked as if a gust of wind might blow him over, had an iron will, a fierce fighting spirit, and a modern rational mind. On stage this supple, graceful actor gave a determined performance, working until all those watching were drawn in by his spell. Audiences were caught unawares by this disparity between the actor's outward appearance and his inner strength, impressed by his spirit, and finally enchanted. The dramatic space Utaemon created was intense, as if he were behind closed doors with his audience, ensnaring each one of them and reeling them in by a separate thread. This is how Utaemon struggled with a postwar era that was a mixture of freedom and in-your-face licentiousness.

Tamasaburō appeared in an age that was already international, soaring onto the stage like a comet, surprising and eventually charming audiences with a refreshing sense of freedom and an airy androgynous presence never before seen in an *onnagata*. With his long body and small face this *onnagata* has a typically Japanese physique, and yet at the same time brims with an unfettered beauty not constrained by his roots in the small islands of Japan. Tamasaburō has in fact taken a variety of acting roles elsewhere, including playing the parts of Desdemona and La Traviata, and others. Referring to this freedom of spirit someone once said that Tamasaburō was from another planet, and it is true that the *onnagata* beauty of Tamasaburō, while unmistakably part of the world of Kabuki, is a beauty in its own right that radiates the same intensity in the world outside of Kabuki.

We must not lose sight of the fact that the "beauty" which Tamasaburō creates is a beauty firmly rooted in the acting traditions of Kabuki.

第二次大戦後の、半世紀に余る歌舞伎の歩みの中で、代表的な女形を二人挙げろと言われたなら、中村歌右衛門と坂東玉三郎ということになるだろう。名女形＝女形の名優という意味でなら、他にも幾人かの名前がすぐに思いつくが、それぞれに時代を映し、時代と対峙しながら独自の美の世界を作り上げたという意味でいうなら、この二人を措いてはない。

歌右衛門は、大戦直後の世代交代と共に台頭し、いわゆる戦後歌舞伎を支えたビッグ6の一人であり、同世代のもう一人の名女形尾上梅幸と並び称されたが、その人々の中でも最も鮮烈に、社会の価値観や美意識が大きく変動した困難な時代の状況と切り結びながら、この人ならではの美の世界を舞台上に現出して、人々を魅了した。見た目には細く、華奢で、今にも折れてしまいそうな古風な容姿の陰に、強い意志と、激しい闘志と、近代的な合理精神を宿していた「彼」は、たおやかで嫋々とした舞台姿で、見る者を説得しなければ止まぬ意志的な演技を見せた。人々はその懸隔に驚き、その気迫に打たれ、やがて虜になった。彼の作り出す演劇空間は、密室のように濃密で、目に見えぬ一筋一筋の糸で見る者をからめ取るかのようだった。歌右衛門はそうした仕方で、大戦後の白々とした、自由と放恣が混在したような時代と戦ったのである。

玉三郎は、国際化した時代に、彗星のように登場し、それまでの歌舞伎の女形にはない新鮮で自由な感覚と、両性具有的な軽やかな存在感で人々を驚かせ、やがて魅了した。長身で顔の小さいその女形姿は、日本的でもありながら、在来の狭い島国意識に縛られない自在な美しさに溢れ、事実彼は、歌舞伎ばかりでなく、デズデモーナや椿姫を演じたり、多彩な活動を見せた。ある人はその自在さを評して、彼は宇宙人だと言ったが、たしかに、玉三郎の女形の美の世界は、紛れもなく歌舞伎でもありながら、同時に、歌舞伎の外の世界へも、それが美しいものである限り、同じ密度で開かれているのである。

しかし、見落としてはならないのは、そうした玉三郎の作り出す「美」が、あくまで歌舞伎の芸をしっかり踏まえた上に生み出されていることである。

代表する女形

中村歌右衛門 Nakamura Utaemon

137

坂東玉三郎 Bandō Tamasaburō

Odori: Kabuki Dance

As the word *ka* (song) -*bu* (dance) and -*ki* (play) indicates, dance is an important element of Kabuki. All Kabuki actors undergo dance training in their youth as part of their basic preparation for the theater. This is because even if he does not actually dance on stage, every aspect of how an actor carries himself during a performance will depend on his training in dance.

There are various categories of dance in Kabuki, and many dance pieces. Most Kabuki programs include one or two dance performances. We use the general term "dance" here, but the "*sambasō*," with their strong ceremonial overtones, and the *Nōtorimono*—Kabuki versions of Nō—are mainly of the *mai* variety of dance. *Mai* dancing chiefly involves revolving in a circle by sliding the feet along the floor.

Most Kabuki dance consists of freer and more worldly dancing. In "Musume Dōjōji," for example, at the beginning of the play a dignified dance modeled on the dance of Nō pays homage to Kabuki's origins in Nō. When this prelude has concluded, the dancing turns into that of Kabuki as the various poses and phases of the love of a young woman unfold like a musical suite. This is a good example of the dance of Kabuki as a descendant of Nō.

Short dances such as "Fuji Musume" (Wisteria Maiden) and "Ukare Bōzu" (Mischievous Priest) that sketch the common people of the streets are the most popular remnants of suites of dances depicting people of varying statuses and occupations, performed in succession. "Seki no To" (Love at the Osaka Barrier) is one example of the plays at the beginning and end of what was originally a long program being lost and only the dance sequence remaining as a piece in its own right. Naturally the story becomes somewhat vague in the process, but the fascination of the dance itself overcomes this to make "Seki no To" a popular feature of the Kabuki repertoire today.

踊り

歌・舞・伎という言葉が示すように、舞踊は歌舞伎を支える重要な要素である。歌舞伎俳優である以上、誰でも、基礎的な素養として若い時に踊りの稽古をしない者はいない。舞台で特に踊るわけでなくとも、演技の中の身のこなしひとつにも、抜き差しがたく舞踊の素養のあるなしが物を言うからである。

また歌舞伎には、ジャンルとしての舞踊があり、多数の演目がある。一興行分の演目のメニューの中に、大概、ひとつふたつ、舞踊の作品が混じえられる。

一口に舞踊というが、『三番叟』のような式楽性の強いものや、能を歌舞伎化した「能取り物」は、「舞い」を主体にしたものが多い。舞いとは、摺り足で旋回する動きを主体とする。

しかし歌舞伎舞踊の多くは、もっと自由で現世的な、「踊り」を主体としたものである。『娘道成寺』のように、冒頭の部分だけは「本行」(原典)である能に敬意を表して能に倣って荘重に舞うが、その、いわば前奏曲がすむと、後は歌舞伎風の踊りになって、若い女性のさまざまな姿体や恋心の相を組曲のように見せて行くのは、能楽の子孫である歌舞伎の踊りの特徴をよく現わしている。

『藤娘』や『うかれ坊主』のような、市井の庶民の姿のスケッチのような短編の踊りは、本来、さまざまな身分や職業の姿を組曲に作って、次々と踊り分けたものの中から、人気曲として今に残ったものである。『関の扉』などの場合は、本来長篇の劇の前後の芝居の部分が伝承されず、踊りの場面だけが一幕物として残ったものである。当然、ストーリーは不得要領になるが、それを超えたパフォーマンスとしての面白さが、今もこの曲を人気レパートリーの中に残しているのである。

Renjishi 連獅子

Music

It is possible to think of Kabuki as a kind of musical theater, and four types of music—the *nagauta*, *takemoto*, *kiyomoto*, and *tokiwazu*—underpin the Kabuki performance. The *nagauta*, or epic ballad, in particular plays a central role.

The *nagauta* is performed using a *hosozao* (narrow-necked) *shamisen* with a clear, high-pitched tone, and is accompanied by an ensemble, known as a *hayashi*, consisting of three kinds of drum (a small *kotsuzumi* drum played on the shoulder, an *ōtsuzumi*, a larger drum played at the waist, and a *taiko* played using two sticks), and a flute. During a dance performance, the *nagauta* and *shamisen* musicians on the top and the *hayashi* on the bottom tier of a stand covered with red carpet are visible to all at the back of the stage facing the audience. The most important job of *nagauta* musicians, in a "secret corner" at stage right known as the *geza* or *kuromisu*, is to perform the background music and sound effects to coincide with the action on stage.

The *takemoto* is the Kabuki name for what in *Ningyō jōruri* (doll theater) is known as the *gidayū*, or narrator. His most important role is that of the narrator of *gidayū kyōgen* or *maruhonmono* plays adapted from the *jōruri* or literary content of Bunraku. Each narrator tells his story to the accompaniment of a low-pitched *futozao*, or wide-necked *shamisen*.

Kiyomoto and *tokiwazu* music are chiefly used to accompany dancing. The freely expanding and contracting high-pitched sounds of the *kiyomoto* are often employed in *nureba* (literally "wet scenes," or love scenes) and are effective in building up mood. *Tokiwazu* tend to be major songs with a story to tell, such as "Seki no To" and "Masakado," or small humorous pieces.

音楽

歌舞伎は一種の音楽劇と考えることも可能だが、「長唄」「竹本」「清元」「常磐津」という四種類のジャンルが、歌舞伎を支えている。特に長唄は最も中心的な役割を果たしている。

長唄は、高音で歯切れのよい音色を持つ「細棹」の三味線と、鼓・大鼓・太鼓・笛の四つの楽器で編成する「囃子」の伴奏で唄う。踊りの時に舞台正面の奥に緋毛氈を二段に敷いた雛段に、上段に長唄と三味線、下段に囃子が並んで演奏するのが誰の目にもつくが、長唄のもうひとつの重要な任務は、舞台下手に設置された「下座」または「黒御簾」と呼ぶ陰のコーナーで、芝居の進行に添ってBGMや効果音を演奏することである。

「竹本」は人形浄瑠璃＝文楽の語り手である「義太夫」の歌舞伎における名称である。浄瑠璃を歌舞伎化した「義太夫狂言」または「丸本物」の語り手役が最も重要な任務である。低音の利く「太棹」の三味線と、一人一挺で語る。

「清元」と「常磐津」は主に舞踊の伴奏をつとめる。清元の伸縮自在な高音は、よく「濡れ場」（ラブシーン）に使われ、情趣をかき立てるのが印象的である。「常磐津」は『関の扉』『将門』など、ストーリー性のある大曲や、滑稽味のある小品が多い。

積恋雪関扉

Tsumoru Koi Yuki no Seki no To

Costume: **B**ukkaeri

In Kabuki the costumes are more than simply clothing; costumes are part of the performance.

In "Seki no To," for example, at the beginning the main character is disguised as the lowly mountain woodcutter Sekibei, but when his true identity as the evil Ōtomo no Kuronushi, who has plans for usurping the throne, is revealed, threads on strategic points of his costume are pulled out and the body of it turns inside out in a single movement, transforming it into the black *sokutai* (court dress) of a high-ranking court noble. By changing his costume in an instant, the true nature of the man disguised as a humble peasant becomes obvious to all.

衣裳
ぶっ返り

歌舞伎の衣裳は単なる衣類ではない。衣裳もまた、演技をする。
たとえば『関の扉』で、はじめ身分の卑しい樵の関兵衛に身をやつして(偽って)いる時の衣裳が、実は彼が天下簒奪を担う大悪人大伴黒主という本性を現わす時、衣裳の要所要所の糸を抜くと、ボディの部分が一挙に裏返って、黒の束帯という堂上公卿(身分の高い宮廷貴族)の衣裳に変る。衣裳を一瞬にして変化させることによって、卑しい身分の男に隠していた本性を、視覚上からも顕現させるのだ。

Iromoyō Chotto Karimame
色彩間苅豆
Kasane
かさね

藤娘 Fuji Musume

土蜘 Tsuchigumo

Funa Benkei
船弁慶

京鹿子娘道成寺

Kyōganoko Musume Dōjōji

Costume: *Hikinuki*

衣裳引抜き

In "Kyōganoko Musume Dōjōji," one of the most notable pieces of music in Kabuki dance, the various phases of a young woman's love are presented in a musical suite. Each change in phase suggests a change of heart. The dancer also changes costume for each new phase. While the color of the costume changes, the pattern does not, although there may be slight variations. In other words, a single costume appears to change with each phase of the dance. To achieve this effect a *kōken*, or assistant, pulls a thread on the costume as the dancer moves, whereupon the costume visible up to that point peels away to reveal one of a different color underneath. At the same time the music enters a new phase and the audience has the sensation of being part of a rapidly changing dream.

In the dance "Sagi Musume" (Heron Maiden), a young girl burning with obsessive desire and transformed into a heron pulls off her layers of costume one after the other midway through the dance to become a gaily dressed girl of the city, almost as if fantasizing about the love that gave her so much joy.

『京鹿子娘道成寺』という歌舞伎舞踊屈指の大曲は、恋をする若い女性のさまざまな相を組曲のように次々と見せて行く。相の変化が心の変化を暗示する。踊り手は、曲の局面局面で衣裳を変えるが、色は変わっても柄は変わらない。多少のヴァリエーションはあるが。つまりひとつの衣裳が、局面の変化につれていろいろに変化するように見える。その効果を現わすために、踊り手は踊り続けながら、後見（助手）が衣裳の糸を抜くと、それまで見えていた衣裳がはがれるように落ちて、下から別の色の衣裳が現われる。同時に曲調が変わる。観客は次々と移り変わる夢を見ているような思いになる。

『鷺娘』という踊りでは、恋の妄執に鷺の化身となった娘が、中段で、次々と衣裳を引き抜いて華やかな町娘になる。まるで、幸せだった恋の思い出を幻想するかのように見える。

Hanagata: The Youngest Generation of Actors

Current stars in the Kabuki galaxy range over several generations, from true veterans of the stage still playing princesses and young girls in their eighties to the youngest actors around the age of twenty.

Ichikawa Shinnosuke, Onoe Kikunosuke, and Onoe Tatsunosuke have been good friends and rivals since childhood, and due to the similarity of their stage names have been collectively dubbed the *sannosuke*, the "three sukes." This was actually the name given to their fathers as young men when they first rose to fame about thirty years ago. Going back further, around half a century or more, their grandfathers were also a youthful trio bound together by good-natured rivalry. This three-actor combination spanning three generations also attracts three generations of supporters, from grandparents to grandchildren. Tradition thrives among Kabuki audiences too.

Stars Nakamura Hashinosuke and Kataoka Takatarō are a little older than the *sannosuke* and therefore more sure of their abilities, and each is steadily carving out a niche for himself in the Kabuki world. Hashinosuke has an impressive pedigree: his great uncle is Nakamura Utaemon, the greatest *onnagata* since WWII; his father, veteran *onnagata* Nakamura Shikan; and older brother, Nakamura Fukusuke, one of the most active *onnagata* today. Takatarō is the son of Kataoka Nizaemon, one of the best *nimaime* actors currently on the Kabuki stage. Hashinosuke has made his name playing *nimaime* characters, while Takatarō specializes in *onnagata* roles.

Ichikawa Somegorō is the son of Matsumoto Kōshirō, who in addition to being a Kabuki actor made a name for himself starring in musicals, performing in English in "Man of La Mancha" on Broadway and "The King and I" in London. Like his father, Somegorō does not limit himself to Kabuki but is also an enthusiastic performer in newer forms of theater.

Brothers Nakamura Kantarō and Shichinosuke are still in their teens (as of March 2001). Their late grandfather Nakamura Kanzaburō, and father Nakamura Kankurō, who is still active, have bequeathed to them the true nature and outstanding technical skill of the Kabuki actor, as the inheritors of a line of acting geniuses, and both brothers are already remarkably similar to their father and grandfather.

These will be the actors sustaining Kabuki in twenty and thirty years time.

歌舞伎界にはいま、80歳を過ぎても姫や娘の役を演じ続けている大ベテランから、20歳前後の最も若い世代まで、幾つもの年齢の層をなしてスター達が存在する。

市川新之助・尾上菊之助・尾上辰之助の三人は、幼い頃からのよき友でありライバルで、芸名の音が共通することから三人揃って「三之助」とニックネームで呼ばれる。実はこの呼称は、約30年前、彼らの親たちが若手として売出した頃につけられたものを、そのまま受け継いだのだ。さらに言えば、約半世紀前、彼らの祖父達もまた、良きライバル同士の若手トリオだった。三代にわたるトリオにはまた、祖父母から孫へ、三代にわたって応援し続けているファンもいる。伝統は観客の側にもあるのだ。

中村橋之助と片岡孝太郎は、三之助よりはやや先輩格の、それだけにもっと安定した実力を身につけたスターであり、着実に地位を築きはじめている。橋之助は、第二次大戦後の最大の名女形中村歌右衛門を大伯父に、当代のベテラン女形中村芝翫を父に、現代最も活躍中の女形の一人である中村福助を兄に持つ、サラブレッドである。また孝太郎は、現在随一の二枚目役者片岡仁左衛門を父に持つ。ただし、橋之助は二枚目役を本領とし、孝太郎は女形を専門にしている。

市川染五郎は、歌舞伎と同時にミュージカルスターとして、ブロードウェイで『ラ・マンチャの男』やロンドンで『王様と私』を英語で公演した経験を持つ松本幸四郎の子で、自身も父と同じく、歌舞伎だけでなく新しい演劇にも熱意を燃やしている。

中村勘太郎と七之助の兄弟はまだ十代である。彼らの祖父中村勘三郎も、現在活躍中の父中村勘九郎も、いかにも歌舞伎役者らしいキャラクターと、卓越した技巧を持つ天才肌の家系であり、二人とも、その祖父にも父にも、いま既に、驚くほどよく似ている。

20年後、30年後の歌舞伎は、きっと彼らが支えていることだろう。

Kabuki Revitalized

It may come as a surprise but new Kabuki works are still being written, and naturally these new productions reflect the atmosphere and demands of modern times.

Ichikawa Shinnosuke, current star of the youngest generation of actors, sports a skinhead look offstage. Shinnosuke is at present the focus of a Kabuki boom, a boom he himself created by performing that classic among classics "Sukeroku" and a new version of the "Genji Monogatari" (The Tale of Genji) in the final year of the twentieth century. "The Tale of Genji" is a famous literary classic written one thousand years ago during the Heian court period, but Shinnosuke brought the hero Hikaru Genji to life for modern times in a manner befitting the 21st century.

"Tenshu Monogatari" is a piece written by Izumi Kyōka in 1917 for a different genre—that of romantic theater—but it has been performed by Tamasaburō with a freshness that denies the existence of barriers between Kabuki and other types of theater.

First staged in 2000, "Yume no Nakazō" features the father and son team of Kōshirō and Somegorō, a pair who consistently challenge the conventions of Kabuki. The play is modeled on the life of the first Nakamura Nakazō, the famous actor who forged a new realism in Kabuki two hundred years ago.

With its long history, a return to the format of earlier days in Kabuki can also be a new venture.

Ichikawa Ennosuke, always on the lookout for new challenges, has launched a new genre known as "Super Kabuki," combining the spectacle of Kabuki with modern messages, while Nakamura Kankurō, one of the most ambitious actors on the Kabuki stage, has revived the Nakamura-za Theater run by his forebears in the Edo Period, in the form of a tent on the banks of the Sumida River, from which emerged the culture of Edo. The new theater allows audiences to experience the ambience of the older, smaller theaters that is lost in huge modern concrete constructions, and succeeds in bringing to life the excitement of Edo Kabuki for the year 2000. The "Heisei Nakamura-za," as the theater is known, can be dismantled and rebuilt anywhere in the world.

歌舞伎に新しい風

意外に思う人もあるかも知れないが、歌舞伎はいまでも新しい作品を生み出し続けている。そうして当然ながら、新しく作られ、作り変えられる歌舞伎は、その時代その時代の空気や、時代の求めるものを反映している。

現代最も若い世代のスターである市川新之助は、素顔は頭をスキンヘッドにしている。彼はいまブームの渦中にいるが、20世紀最後の年、彼は古典中の古典『助六』と新しい『源氏物語』で自らブームを作ったのだった。『源氏物語』は千年前の王朝時代に書かれた古典文学の名作だが、主人公光源氏を新之助は21世紀の感覚で現代に蘇らせた。

『天守物語』は泉鏡花によって近代（大正6年、1917年）に作られた異ジャンルのロマン劇だが、玉三郎はそれを歌舞伎と他ジャンルの間の壁など存在しないかのように、新鮮な感覚で演じた。

『夢の仲蔵』は、幸四郎と染五郎という既成の歌舞伎の枠に捕われない活動を続けている父子が、200年昔に新しいリアリズム劇を創始した名優、初代中村仲蔵をモデルに、「演劇としての歌舞伎」を世に問おうと試みた新作である。

長い歴史を持つ歌舞伎では、昔の姿に帰ることも新しい試みである。常に新しい挑戦を続けている市川猿之助は、歌舞伎のスペクタクル性と現代的なメッセージをミックスした「スーパー歌舞伎」という新ジャンルを開始した。また最も意欲的な俳優の一人である中村勘九郎は、江戸の文化を生んだ母なる川である隅田川の畔に、彼の先祖が経営していた中村座をテント形式で復興し、コンクリート製の近代建築の大劇場が失った、昔の芝居小屋の持っていた臨場感を取り戻し、西暦2000年に江戸の歌舞伎の活気を甦らせることに成功した。「平成中村座」は、解体して世界中どこへでも立てられる構造になっている。

Genji Monogatari 源氏物語

天守物語
Tenshu Monogatari

Yume no Nakazō
夢の仲蔵

181

List of Photographs

p. 1
Kagamijishi
Kikugorō as Shishi no Sei
鏡獅子（獅子の精＝菊五郎）
(6/1988 Kabuki-za 歌舞伎座)

pp. 2–3
Gosho no Gorozō
Kikugorō as Gorozō; Gonjurō III as Doemon
御所五郎蔵（五郎蔵＝菊五郎、土右衛門＝三世権十郎）
(2/1992 Kabuki-za 歌舞伎座)

pp. 4–5
"Yoshinogawa" in *Imoseyama Onna Teikin*
Tokizō as Koganosuke; Shibajaku as Hinadori
妹背山婦女庭訓・吉野川（久我之助＝時蔵、雛鳥＝芝雀）
(11/1996 National Theatre 国立劇場)

p. 6
Shōfudatsuki Kongen Kusazuri
Shinnosuke as Soga no Gorō; Tatsunosuke as Asahina
正札附根元草摺（曽我五郎＝新之助、朝比奈＝辰之助）
(5/1996 Kabuki-za 歌舞伎座)

p. 12
"Michiyuki Tabiji no Hanamuko" in *Kanadehon Chūshingura*
Danjūrō as Kampei; Tamasaburō as Okaru
仮名手本忠臣蔵・道行旅路の花婿（勘平＝團十郎、お軽＝玉三郎）
(4/1989 Kabuki-za 歌舞伎座)

pp. 14–15
Sakura-hime Azuma Bunshō
Tamasaburō as Sakura-hime; Nizaemon as Gonsuke
桜姫東文章（桜姫＝玉三郎、権助＝片岡仁左衛門）
(3/1981 Kabuki-za 歌舞伎座)

p. 16
Ehon Ushiwakamaru
Kikugorō; Kikunosuke
絵本牛若丸（菊五郎、菊之助）
(2/1984 Kabuki-za 歌舞伎座)

pp. 18–19
Ehon Ushiwakamaru
Kikugorō; Kikunosuke; Baikō VII
絵本牛若丸（尾上菊五郎・尾上菊之助・七世尾上梅幸）
(2/1984 Kabuki-za 歌舞伎座)

p. 20
Ehon Ushiwakamaru
絵本牛若丸
(2/1984 Kabuki-za 歌舞伎座)

p. 21
Hirakana Seisuiki
ひらかな盛衰記
(11/1984 National Theatre 国立劇場)

"Terakoya" in *Sugawara Denju Tenarai Kagami*
菅原伝授手習鑑・寺子屋
(5/1985 Kabuki-za 歌舞伎座)

Kyōganoko Musume Dōjōji
京鹿子娘道成寺
(3/1985 National Theatre 国立劇場)

p. 22
Uirō Uri
外郎売
(5/1985 Kabuki-za 歌舞伎座)

p. 23
Kagamijishi
鏡獅子
(6/1988 Kabuki-za 歌舞伎座)

Kasane Ōgi Yukari no Ekurabe
重扇縁絵競
(2/1989 Kabuki-za 歌舞伎座)

p. 24
Jitsuroku Sendai Hagi
実録先代萩
(3/1987 National Theatre 国立劇場)

p. 25
"Michiyuki Tabiji no Yomeiri" in *Kanadehon Chūshingura*
仮名手本忠臣蔵・道行旅路の嫁入
(4/1993 Meiji-za 明治座)

p. 26
Yowa Nasake Ukina no Yokogushi
與話情浮名横櫛
(9/1985 Kōriyama Shimin Bunka Center 郡山市民文化センター)

"Yamashina Kankyo" in *Kanadehon Chūshingura*
仮名手本忠臣蔵・山科閑居
(2/1997 Kabuki-za 歌舞伎座)

p. 27
Kyōganoko Musume Sannin Dōjōji
Kikugorō as Sakurako; Baikō VII as Hanako; Kikunosuke as Otowa
京鹿子娘三人道成寺（桜子＝菊五郎、花子＝七世梅幸、音羽＝菊之助）
(11/1992 Kabuki-za 歌舞伎座)

p. 28
Sukeroku Yukari no Edo-zakura
助六由縁江戸桜
(4/1985 Kabuki-za 歌舞伎座)

p. 29
Sukeroku Yukari no Edo-zakura
助六由縁江戸桜
(1/2000 Shimbashi Embu-jō 新橋演舞場)

p. 30
Benten Musume Meo no Shiranami
弁天娘女男白浪
(4/1993 Meiji-za 明治座)

p. 31
Benten Musume Meo no Shiranami
弁天娘女男白浪
(1/2000 Shimbashi Embu-jō 新橋演舞場)

p. 32
Benten Musume Meo no Shiranami
弁天娘女男白浪
(1/1995 Kabuki-za 歌舞伎座)

Benten Musume Meo no Shiranami
弁天娘女男白浪
(1/2000 Shimbashi Embu-jō 新橋演舞場)

p. 33
Benten Musume Meo no Shiranami
弁天娘女男白浪
(3/1984 National Theatre 国立劇場)

Benten Musume Meo no Shiranami
弁天娘女男白浪
(1/2000 Shimbashi Embu-jō 新橋演舞場)

p. 34
"Kuruma-biki" in *Sugawara Denju Tenarai Kagami*
菅原伝授手習鑑・車引
(top, 3/2000 Kabuki-za 歌舞伎座)
(bottom, 5/1993 Kabuki-za 歌舞伎座)

p. 35
"Jusshu Kō" in *Honchō Nijūshi Kō*
本朝廿四孝・十種香
(left, 3/1999 Kabuki-za 歌舞伎座)
(right, 5/2000 Kabuki-za 歌舞伎座)

pp. 36–37
Benten Musume Meo no Shiranami
Danjūrō as Nippondaemon; Kikugorō as Benten Kozō; Mitsugorō as Tadanobu; Hikosaburō as Nangō; Manjirō as Akaboshi
弁天娘女男白浪（日本駄右衛門＝團十郎、弁天小僧＝菊五郎、忠信＝三津五郎、南郷＝彦三郎、赤星＝萬次郎）
(1/1985 Asakusa Kōkaidō 浅草公会堂)

p. 38
Gosho no Gorozō
Kikugorō as Gorozō
御所五郎蔵（五郎蔵＝菊五郎）
(1/1999 Kabuki-za 歌舞伎座)

p. 39
Sukeroku Yukari no Edo-zakura
Kikunosuke as Shiratama
助六由縁江戸桜（白玉＝菊之助）
(1/2000 Shimbashi Embu-jō)

p. 40
Funa Benkei
Kikugorō as Taira no Tomomori no Rei
船弁慶（平知盛の霊＝菊五郎）
(5/1998 Kabuki-za 歌舞伎座)

Onna Shibaraku
Kikugorō as Tomoe Gozen
女暫（巴御前＝菊五郎）
(2/1998 Kabuki-za)

p. 41
Ichijō Ōkura Monogatari
Kantarō as Ichijō Ōkura-kyō
一條大蔵譚（一條大蔵卿＝勘太郎）
(1/2001 Asakusa Kōkaidō 浅草公会堂)

p. 43
Shibaraku (Gohiiki Kanjinchō)
Kikugorō as Kumai no Tarō Tadamoto
御摂勧進帳・暫（熊井太郎忠基＝菊五郎）
(1/1988 National Theatre 国立劇場)

p. 44
Sukeroku Yukari no Edo-zakura
Danjūrō as Sukeroku; Kikugorō as Agemaki
助六由縁江戸桜（助六＝團十郎、揚巻＝菊五郎）
(6/1985 Kabuki-za 歌舞伎座)

p. 45
Sukeroku Yukari no Edo-zakura
Danjūrō as Sukeroku
助六由縁江戸桜（助六＝團十郎）
(6/1985 Kabuki-za 歌舞伎座)

p. 46
Sukeroku Yukari no Edo-zakura
Shinnosuke as Sukeroku
助六由縁江戸桜（助六＝新之助）
(1/2000 Shimbashi Embu-jō 新橋演舞場)

p. 47
Sukeroku Yukari no Edo-zakura
Shinnosuke as Sukeroku, Sadanji as Ikyū
助六由縁江戸桜（助六＝新之助、意休＝左團次）
(1/2000 Shimbashi Embu-jō 新橋演舞場)

p. 48
Sukeroku Kuruwa no Momoyogusa
Kikugorō as Sukeroku; Gonjurō III as Ikyū
助六曲輪菊（助六＝菊五郎、意休＝三世権十郎）
(11/1989 Kabuki-za 歌舞伎座)

p. 49
Sukeroku Yukari no Edo-zakura
Shinnosuke as Sukeroku
助六由縁江戸桜（助六＝新之助）
(1/2000 Shimbashi Embu-jō 新橋演舞場)

p. 50
Kanjinchō
Shinnosuke as Benkei; Kikunosuke as Yoshitsune
勧進帳（弁慶＝新之助、義経＝菊之助）
(1/1999 Asakusa Kōkaidō 浅草公会堂)

p. 51
Kanjinchō
Danjūrō as Benkei
勧進帳（弁慶＝團十郎）
(5/1986 Kabuki-za 歌舞伎座)

p. 52
Kanjinchō
top, Tatsunosuke as Benkei; Shinnosuke as Togashi
(1/1998 Asakusa Kōkaidō 浅草公会堂)
bottom, Shinnosuke as Benkei
(1/1999 Asakusa Kōkaidō 浅草公会堂)
勧進帳（写真上：弁慶＝辰之助、富樫＝新之助　写真下：弁慶＝新之助）

pp. 53–54
Kanjinchō
Shinnosuke as Benkei
勧進帳（弁慶＝新之助）
(1/1999 Asakusa Kōkaidō 浅草公会堂)

pp. 55–57
Narukami
Nizaemon as Narukami Shōnin; Tamasaburō as Kumo no Taema-hime
鳴神（鳴神上人＝仁左衛門、雲の絶間姫＝玉三郎）
(9/1981 Kabuki-za 歌舞伎座)

p. 58
Kōshirō with *kumadori* makeup
化粧−隈取（幸四郎）

p. 59
Kikugorō applying *kumadori* makeup
暫の化粧（菊五郎）

p. 60
Kikugorō putting on *Shibaraku* costume
暫のこしらえ（菊五郎）

pp. 62–63
Shibaraku (Gohiiki Kanjinchō)
Kikugorō as Kumai no Tarō Tadamoto
御摂勧進帳・暫（熊井太郎忠基＝菊五郎）
(1/1988 National Theatre 国立劇場)

p. 65
Kanadehon Chūshingura
top, Act 3
bottom, Act 4
Kikugorō as Enya Hangan
仮名手本忠臣蔵・三段目、四段目（塩治判官＝菊五郎）
(4/1988 Kabuki-za 歌舞伎座)

p. 66
"Michiyuki Tabiji no Hanamuko" in *Kanadehon Chūshingura*
Tomijūrō as Kampei; Kikugorō as Okaru
仮名手本忠臣蔵・道行旅路の花婿（勘平＝富十郎、お軽＝菊五郎）
(1/1996 Kabuki-za 歌舞伎座)

p. 67
"Michiyuki Tabiji no Hanamuko" in *Kanadehon Chūshingura*
top, Kikugorō as Kampei; Tokizō as Okaru; Tatsunosuke as Bannai
bottom, Kikugorō as Kampei
仮名手本忠臣蔵・道行旅路の花婿（勘平＝菊五郎、お軽＝時蔵、伴内＝辰之助）
(3/1998 Kabuki-za 歌舞伎座)

p. 68
Kanadehon Chūshingura
Act 5
top, Kikugorō as Kampei; Fukusuke as Okaru
(3/1998 Kabuki-za 歌舞伎座)
bottom, Kikugorō as Kampei; Tamasaburō as Okaru
(4/1988 Kabuki-za 歌舞伎座)
仮名手本忠臣蔵・五段目（写真上：勘平＝菊五郎、お軽＝福助　写真下：勘平＝菊五郎、お軽＝玉三郎）

p. 69
Kanadehon Chūshingura
Act 5
top, Hashinosuke as Sadakurō
bottom, Kikugorō as Kampei
仮名手本忠臣蔵・五段目（写真上：定九郎＝橋之助　写真下：勘平＝菊五郎）
(3/1998 Kabuki-za 歌舞伎座)

p. 70
Kanadehon Chūshingura
Act 6
Kikugorō as Kampei
仮名手本忠臣蔵・六段目（勘平＝菊五郎）
(3/1998 Kabuki-za 歌舞伎座)

p. 71
Kanadehon Chūshingura
Act 7
Tamasaburō as Okaru
仮名手本忠臣蔵・七段目（お軽＝玉三郎）
(3/1998 Kabuki-za 歌舞伎座)

pp. 72–73
Act 9
"Yamashina Kankyo" in *Kanadehon Chūshingura*
Kikugorō as Tonase; Kikunosuke as Konami
仮名手本忠臣蔵・九段目（戸無瀬＝菊五郎、小浪＝菊之助）
(2/1997 Kabuki-za 歌舞伎座)

p. 74
"Kamotsuzumi" in *Sugawara Denju Tenarai Kagami*
top, Kikugorō as Sakuramaru; Ganjirō as Yae
bottom, Fukusuke as Kariya-hime; Kankurō as Prince Tokiyo
菅原伝授手習鑑・加茂堤（写真上：桜丸＝菊五郎、八重＝鴈治郎　写真下：苅屋姫＝福助、斎世親王＝勘九郎）
(2/1988 Kabuki-za 歌舞伎座)

p. 75
"Kuruma-biki" in *Sugawara Denju Tenarai Kagami*
Kōshirō as Matsuōmaru
菅原伝授手習鑑・車引（松王丸＝幸四郎）
(3/2000 Kabuki-za 歌舞伎座)

p. 76
"Kuruma-biki" in *Sugawara Denju Tenarai Kagami*
Kikugorō as Sakuramaru
菅原伝授手習鑑・車引（桜丸＝菊五郎）
(3/2000 Kabuki-za 歌舞伎座)

p. 77
"Kuruma-biki" in *Sugawara Denju Tenarai Kagami*
Danjūrō as Umeōmaru
菅原伝授手習鑑・車引（梅王丸＝團十郎）
(3/2000 Kabuki-za 歌舞伎座)

pp. 78–79
"Kuruma-biki" in *Sugawara Denju Tenarai Kagami*
Kikugorō as Sakuramaru; Kōshirō as Matsuōmaru; Danjūrō as Umeōmaru; Hikosaburō as Shihei
菅原伝授手習鑑・車引（桜丸＝菊五郎、松王丸＝幸四郎、梅王丸＝團十郎、時平＝彦三郎）
(3/2000 Kabuki-za 歌舞伎座)

p. 80
"Ga no Iwai" in *Sugawara Denju Tenarai Kagami*
Kōshirō as Matsuōmaru; Danjūrō as Umeōmaru
菅原伝授手習鑑・賀の祝（松王丸＝幸四郎、梅王丸＝團十郎）
(3/2000 Kabuki-za 歌舞伎座)

p. 81
"Ga no Iwai" in *Sugawara Denju Tenarai Kagami*
Tokizō as Yae; Kikugorō as Sakuramaru
菅原伝授手習鑑・賀の祝（八重＝時蔵、桜丸＝菊五郎）
(3/2000 Kabuki-za 歌舞伎座)

pp. 82–83
"Terakoya" in *Sugawara Denju Tenarai Kagami*
Kōshirō as Matsuōmaru
菅原伝授手習鑑・寺子屋（松王丸＝幸四郎）
(3/1997 Kabuki-za 歌舞伎座)

p. 84
"Sushiya" in *Yoshitsune Sembonzakura*
Kōshirō as Gonta
義経千本桜・すし屋（権太＝幸四郎）
(6/1996 Kabuki-za 歌舞伎座)

p. 85
"Sushiya" in *Yoshitsune Sembonzakura*
Kikugorō as Gonta
義経千本桜・すし屋（権太＝菊五郎）
(6/1986 Kabuki-za 歌舞伎座)

p. 86
"Kawatsura Hōgen Yakata" in *Yoshitsune Sembonzakura*
義経千本桜・河連法眼館（忠信＝菊五郎）
Kikugorō as Tadanobu
(5/1995 Kabuki-za 歌舞伎座)

p. 87
"Kawatsura Hōgen Yakata" in *Yoshitsune Sembonzakura*
義経千本桜・河連法眼館（源九郎狐＝菊五郎）
Kikugorō as Genkurō Kitsune
(5/1995 Kabuki-za 歌舞伎座)

pp. 88–89
"Kawatsura Hōgen Yakata" in *Yoshitsune Sembonzakura*
Kikugorō as Genkurō Kitsune; Shibajaku as Shizuka Gozen; Mitsugorō as Yoshitsune
義経千本桜・河連法眼館（源九郎狐＝菊五郎、静御前＝芝雀、義経＝三津五郎）
(5/1995 Kabuki-za 歌舞伎座)

p. 90
"Hana Watashi" in *Imoseyama Onna Teikin*
Mitsugorō IX as Soga no Iruka
妹背山婦女庭訓・花渡し（入鹿＝九世三津五郎）
(11/1996 National Theatre 国立劇場)

p. 91
"Yoshinogawa" in *Imoseyama Onna Teikin*
top, Tokizō as Koganosuke; Shibajaku as Hinadori
bottom, Kōshirō as Daihanji
妹背山婦女庭訓・吉野川（写真上：久我之助＝時蔵、雛鳥＝芝雀　写真下：大判事＝幸四郎）
(11/1996 National Theatre 国立劇場)

pp. 92–93
"Michiyuki Koi no Odamaki" in *Imoseyama Onna Teikin*
Kikunosuke as Tachibana-hime; Tatsunosuke as Motome; Jakuemon as Omiwa
妹背山婦女庭訓・道行恋苧環（橘姫＝菊之助、求女＝辰之助、お三輪＝雀右衛門）
(11/1996 National Theatre 国立劇場)

pp. 94–95
"Kumiuchi" in *Ichinotani Futaba Gunki*
Kōshirō as Kumagai; Somegorō as Kojirō
一谷嫩軍記・組内（熊谷直実＝幸四郎、小次郎＝染五郎）
(2/1996 Kabuki-za 歌舞伎座)

pp. 96–97
"Kumagai Jinya" in *Ichinotani Futaba Gunki*
Kōshirō as Kumagai; Kikugorō as Yoshitsune
一谷嫩軍記・熊谷陣屋（熊谷直実＝幸四郎、義経＝菊五郎）
(2/1996 Kabuki-za 歌舞伎座)

pp. 98–99
Ichijō Ōkura Monogatari
Kantarō as Ichijō Ōkura-kyō
一條大蔵譚（一條大蔵卿＝勘太郎）
(1/2001 Asakusa Kōkaidō 浅草公会堂)

pp. 100–101
Meiboku Sendai Hagi
Kikugorō as Masaoka; Gonjurō III as Yashio
伽羅先代萩（梅照葉錦伊達織、政岡＝菊五郎、八汐＝三世権十郎）
(12/1995 National Theatre 国立劇場)

pp. 102–103
"Jusshu Kō" in *Honchō Nijūshi Kō*
Shinnosuke as Takeda Katsuyori; Kikunosuke as Yaegaki-hime
本朝廿四孝・十種香（武田勝頼＝新之助、八重垣姫＝菊之助）
(5/2000 Kabuki-za 歌舞伎座)

p. 104
Sanemori Monogatari
top, Gonjurō III as Senō
bottom, Kikugorō as Sanemori; Gonjurō III as Senō
実盛物語（実盛＝菊五郎、瀬尾＝三世権十郎）
(1/1993 National Theatre 国立劇場)

p. 105
Sanemori Monogatari
Kikugorō as Sanemori
実盛物語（実盛＝菊五郎）
(9/1990 Kabuki-za 歌舞伎座)

pp. 106–107
Kuruwa Bunshō
Kanzaburō XVII as Izaemon; Tamasaburō as Yūgiri
廓文章（伊左衛門＝十七世勘三郎、夕霧＝玉三郎）
(1/1979 National Theatre 国立劇場)

pp. 108–109
Benten Musume Meo no Shiranami
Danjūrō as Nippondaemon; Kikugorō as Benten Kozō; Mitsugorō as Tadanobu; Hikosaburō as Nangō; Manjirō as Akaboshi
弁天娘女男白浪（日本駄右衛門＝團十郎、弁天小僧＝菊五郎、忠信＝三津五郎、南郷＝彦三郎、赤星＝萬次郎）
(1/1985 Asakusa Kōkaidō 浅草公会堂)

pp. 110–113
Kagotsurube Sato no Eizame
Kōshirō as Jirozaemon; Tamasaburō as Yatsuhashi; Tōjūrō as Kokonoe; Somegorō as Jiroku
籠釣瓶花街酔醒（次郎左衛門＝幸四郎、八ツ橋＝玉三郎、九重＝藤十郎、治六＝染五郎）
(3/1997 Kabuki-za 歌舞伎座)

pp. 114–115
Tōkaidō Yotsuya Kaidan
Kankurō as Oiwa and Yomoshichi; Hashinosuke as Iemon; Mitsugorō as Naosuke
東海道四谷怪談（お岩、与茂七＝勘九郎、伊右衛門＝橋之助、直助＝三津五郎）
(8/2000 Kabuki-za 歌舞伎座)

p. 116
Yowa Nasake Ukina no Yokogushi
Tamasaburō as Otomi
与話情浮名横櫛（お富＝玉三郎）
(5/1977 Kabuki-za 歌舞伎座)

p. 117
Yowa Nasake Ukina no Yokogushi
top, Danjūrō as Yosaburō
(4/1987 Osaka Shin Kabuki-za 大阪新歌舞伎座)
bottom, Kikugorō as Yosaburō; Tamasaburō as Otomi
(5/1977 Kabuki-za 歌舞伎座)
与話情浮名横櫛（写真上：与三郎＝團十郎　写真下：与三郎＝菊五郎、お富＝玉三郎）

pp. 118–119
Yuki no Yūbe Iriya no Azemichi
Kikugorō as Naojirō; Tamasaburō as Michitose
雪暮夜入谷畦道（直次郎＝菊五郎、玉三郎＝三千歳）
(1/1989 National Theatre 国立劇場)

pp. 120–121
Sakura-hime Azuma Bunshō
Tamasaburō as Sakura-hime; Nizaemon as Seigen
桜姫東文章（桜姫＝玉三郎、清玄＝仁左衛門）
(3/1985 Kabuki-za 歌舞伎座)

pp. 122–123
Sakura-hime Azuma Bunshō
Tamasaburō as Sakura-hime; Nizaemon as Gonsuke
桜姫東文章（桜姫＝玉三郎、権助＝仁左衛門）
(1/1981 Kabuki-za 歌舞伎座)

p. 124
Izayoi Seishin
Kikugorō as Seishin; Kikunosuke as Motome
十六夜清心（清心＝菊五郎、求女＝菊之助）
(11/1997 Kabuki-za 歌舞伎座)

p. 125
Izayoi Seishin
Tamasaburō as Izayoi; Kikugorō as Seishin
十六夜清心（十六夜＝玉三郎、清心＝菊五郎）
(12/1986 Kabuki-za 歌舞伎座)

p. 126
Gosho no Gorozō
Kikugorō as Gorozō
御所五郎蔵（五郎蔵＝菊五郎）
(2/1992 Kabuki-za 歌舞伎座)

p. 127
Kajiwara Heizō Homare no Ishikiri
Kōshirō as Kajiwara
梶原平三誉石切（梶原＝幸四郎）
(1/1996 Kabuki-za 歌舞伎座)

p. 128
"Sakaro" in *Hirakana Seisuiki*
Kōshirō as Higuchi
ひらかな盛衰記・逆櫓（樋口＝幸四郎）
(6/1996 Kabuki-za 歌舞伎座)

p. 129
top, *Shin Usuyuki Monogatari*
Kōshirō as Saisaki Iganokami
写真上：新薄雪物語（幸崎伊賀守＝幸四郎）
(6/1997 Kabuki-za 歌舞伎座)
bottom, *Kuruwa Bunshō*
Ganjirō as Izaemon
写真下：廓文章（伊左衛門＝鴈治郎）
(12/1984 Minami-za, Kyoto)

p. 130
"Nozakimura" in *Shimpan Utazaimon*
Tamasaburō as Osome
新版歌祭文・野崎村（お染＝玉三郎）
(1/1979 National Theatre 国立劇場)

p. 131
top, *Sukeroku Yukari no Edo-zakura*
Utaemon as Agemaki
写真上：助六由縁江戸桜（揚巻＝歌右衛門）
(4/1982 Shimbashi Embu-jō 新橋演舞場)
bottom, "Michiyuki Koi no Odamaki" in *Imoseyama Onna Teikin*
Shikan as Tachibana-hime; Jakuemon as Omiwa
写真下：妹背山婦女庭訓・道行恋苧環（橘姫＝芝翫、お三輪＝雀右衛門）
(5/1988 Kabuki-za 歌舞伎座)

pp. 133–134
Kagotsurube Sato no Eizame
Utaemon as Yatsuhashi; Kanzaburō XVII as Jirozaemon
籠釣瓶花街酔醒（八ツ橋＝歌右衛門、次郎左衛門＝十七世勘三郎）
(4/1982 Shimbashi Embu-jō 新橋演舞場)

p. 135
top, *Kagotsurube Sato no Eizame*
Utaemon as Yatsuhashi; Kikugorō as Einojō
写真上：籠釣瓶花街酔醒（八ツ橋＝歌右衛門、栄之丞＝菊五郎）
(4/1982 Shimbashi Embu-jō 新橋演舞場)
bottom, "Genta Kandō" in *Hirakana Seisuiki*
Utaemon as Enju
写真下：ひらかな盛衰記（延寿＝歌右衛門）
(5/1986 Kabuki-za 歌舞伎座)

pp. 136–137
Nihon Furisode Hajime
Utaemon as Iwanaga-hime and Yamata no Orochi; Kikugorō as Inada-hime
日本振袖始（岩永姫、八岐の大蛇＝歌右衛門、稲田姫＝菊五郎）
(5/1984 Kabuki-za 歌舞伎座)

pp. 138–140
Sukeroku Kuruwa no Hatsu-zakura
Tamasaburō as Agemaki; Nizaemon as Sukeroku; Nizaemon XIII as Ikyū
助六曲輪初花桜（揚巻＝玉三郎、助六＝仁左衛門、意休＝十三世仁左衛門）
(3/1983 Kabuki-za 歌舞伎座)

p. 141
Omatsuri
Tamasaburō as Geisha
お祭り（芸者＝玉三郎）
(12/1986 Kabuki-za 歌舞伎座)

pp. 142–143
Kyōganoko Musume Dōjōji
Tamasaburō as Shirabyōshi Hanako
京鹿子娘道成寺（白拍子花子＝玉三郎）
(12/1986 Kabuki-za 歌舞伎座)

pp. 144–145
Kagamijishi
Tamasaburō as Yayoi and Shishi no Sei
鏡獅子（弥生、獅子の精＝玉三郎）
(10/1992 Kabuki-za 歌舞伎座)

pp. 146–149
Renjishi
Kankurō as Kyōgenshi Ukon and Oyajishi no Sei; Kantarō as Kyōgenshi Sakon and Kojishi no Sei
連獅子（狂言師右近、親獅子の精＝勘九郎、狂言師左近、子獅子の精＝勘太郎）
(12/2000 Yokohama 21st Century Theater 横浜21世紀座)

p. 150
Tsumoru Koi Yuki no Seki no To
Kōshirō as Sekibē; Fukusuke as Komachi-hime; Danjūrō as Munesada
積恋雪関扉（関兵衛＝幸四郎、小町姫＝福助、宗貞＝團十郎）
(12/1996 Kabuki-za 歌舞伎座)

p. 151
Tsumoru Koi Yuki no Seki no To
Shikan as Komachi-hime; Kikugorō as Munesada
積恋雪関扉（小町姫＝芝翫、宗貞＝菊五郎）
(1/1999 Kabuki-za 歌舞伎座)

pp. 152–153
Tsumoru Koi Yuki no Seki no To
Kōshirō as Sekibē and Ōtomo no Kuronushi
積恋雪関扉（関兵衛、大伴黒主＝幸四郎）
(12/1996 Kabuki-za 歌舞伎座)

pp. 154–155
Momijigari
Mitsugorō as Ugenta; Kankurō as Sagenta; Fukusuke as Sarashina-hime
紅葉狩（従者・右源太＝三津五郎、従者・左源太＝勘九郎、更級姫＝福助）
(8/2000 Kabuki-za 歌舞伎座)

p. 157
Momijigari
top, Kikugorō as Kijo in Togakushiyama
(11/1988 Kabuki-za 歌舞伎座)
bottom; Fukusuke as Kijo in Togakushiyama; Kashō as Taira no Koremochi
(8/2000 Kabuki-za 歌舞伎座)
紅葉狩（写真上：戸隠山の鬼女＝菊五郎　写真下：戸隠山の鬼女＝福助、平維茂＝歌昇）

pp. 158–159
Kasane
Tamasaburō as Kasane; Nizaemon as Yoemon
かさね（かさね＝玉三郎、与右衛門＝仁左衛門）
(3/1982 Kabuki-za 歌舞伎座)

pp. 160–161
Fuji Musume
Tamasaburō as Fuji Musume
藤娘（藤娘＝玉三郎）
(3/1999 Kabuki-za 歌舞伎座)

pp. 162–163
Tsuchigumo
Kikugorō as Tsuchigumo no Sei and Priest Chichū
土蜘（僧智籌、土蜘の精＝菊五郎）
(6/1993 Shimbashi Embu-jō 新橋演舞場)

p. 164
Funa Benkei
top, Kikugorō as Shizuka Gozen; Danzō as Benkei
(5/1987 Kabuki-za 歌舞伎座)
bottom, Kikugorō as Taira no Tomomori no Rei; Danjūrō as Benkei
(5/1998 Kabuki-za 歌舞伎座)
船弁慶（写真上：静御前＝菊五郎、弁慶＝団蔵　写真下：平知盛の霊＝菊五郎、弁慶＝團十郎）

p. 165
Funa Benkei
Kikugorō as Taira no Tomomori no Rei; Danzō as Benkei
船弁慶（平知盛の霊＝菊五郎、弁慶＝團蔵）
(5/1987 Kabuki-za 歌舞伎座)

pp. 166–168
Kyōganoko Musume Dōjōji
Tamasaburō as Shirabyōshi Hanako
京鹿子娘道成寺（白拍子花子＝玉三郎）
(12/1986 Kabuki-za 歌舞伎座)

p. 169
"Nozakimura" in *Shimpan Utazaimon*
Takatarō as Omitsu
新版歌祭文・野崎村（お光＝孝太郎）
(1/1997 Asakusa Kōkaidō 浅草公会堂)

p. 170 & jacket (front)
Kanjinchō
Shinnosuke as Benkei
勧進帳（弁慶＝新之助）
(1/1999 Asakusa Kōkaidō 浅草公会堂)

p. 171 & jacket (flap)
"Terakoya" in *Sugawara Denju Tenarai Kagami*
Shinnosuke as Matsuōmaru
菅原伝授手習鑑・寺子屋（松王丸＝新之助）
(2/1999 Osaka Shōchiku-za 大阪松竹座)

p. 172
Sukeroku Yukari no Edo-zakura
Kikunosuke as Shiratama
助六由縁江戸桜（白玉＝菊之助）
(1/2000 Shimbashi Embu-jō 新橋演舞場)

p. 173
Rampei Monogurui
Tatsunosuke as Rampei
倭仮名在原系図・蘭平物狂（蘭平＝辰之助）
(11/1999 Kabuki-za 歌舞伎座)

p. 174
Genji Monogatari
Tatsunosuke as Tō no Chūjō
源氏物語（頭の中将＝辰之助）
(5/2000 Kabuki-za 歌舞伎座)

p. 175
Genji Monogatari
Shinnosuke as Hikaru no Kimi; Kikunosuke as Murasaki no Ue
源氏物語（光君＝新之助、紫の上＝菊之助）
(5/2000 Kabuki-za 歌舞伎座)

p. 176
Genji Monogatari
top, Tamasaburō as Fujitsubo
bottom, Shinnosuke as Hikaru no Kimi; Kikunosuke as Murasaki no Ue
源氏物語（写真上：藤壺＝玉三郎　写真下：光君＝新之助、紫の上＝菊之助）
(5/2000 Kabuki-za 歌舞伎座)

p. 177
Genji Monogatari
Shinnosuke as Hikaru no Kimi
源氏物語（光君＝新之助）
(5/2000 Kabuki-za 歌舞伎座)

pp. 178–179
Tenshu Monogatari
Tamasaburō as Tomi-hime; Kikunosuke as Kame-hime; Sadanji as Shu no Bambō; Kichinojō as Shitanaga Uba; Kichiya as Susuki
天守物語（富姫＝玉三郎、亀姫＝菊之助、朱の盤坊＝左團次、舌長姥＝吉之丞、薄＝吉弥）
(3/1999 Kabuki-za 歌舞伎座)

p. 180
Yume no Nakazō
top, Kōshirō as Nakazō I
bottom, Kōshirō as Nakazō I (Oshimodoshi); Somegorō as Danjūrō V (Jatai no Kijo)
夢の仲蔵（写真上：初代中村仲蔵＝幸四郎　写真下：初代中村仲蔵＜押戻＞＝幸四郎、五代目團十郎＜蛇体の鬼女＞＝染五郎）
(9/2000 Nissay Theatre 日生劇場)

p. 181
Yume no Nakazō
Kōshirō as Nakazō I (Sekibē); Somegorō as Danjūrō V (Sumizome)
夢の仲蔵（初代中村仲蔵＜関兵衛＞＝幸四郎、五代目團十郎＜墨染＞＝染五郎）
(9/2000 Nissay Theatre 日生劇場)

pp. 182–183
Yume no Nakazō
Kōshirō as Nakazō I (Oshimodoshi); Somegorō as Danjūrō V (Jatai no Kijo)
夢の仲蔵（初代中村仲蔵＜押戻＞＝幸四郎、五代目團十郎＜蛇体の鬼女＞＝染五郎）
(9/2000 Nissay Theatre 日生劇場)

Jacket (back)
Mitsuningyō
Kikunosuke as Keisei
三人形（傾城＝菊之助）
(11/1998 Kabuki-za 歌舞伎座)

Flap
Kagamijishi
Kikunosuke as Shishi no Sei
鏡獅子（獅子の精＝菊之助）
(5/1996 Kabuki-za 歌舞伎座)

All photographs are reproduced with the cooperation and permission of Shochiku Co., Ltd., the actors and the theaters.

YAGŌ (family stage names)

Akashi-ya	Ōtani Tomoemon
Hamamura-ya	Segawa Kikunojō
Harima-ya	Nakamura Kichiemon Nakamura Matagorō
Kaga-ya	Nakamura Matsue Nakamura Tōzō
Kinokuni-ya	Sawamura Tanosuke Sawamura Tōjūrō
Kōrai-ya	Matsumoto Kōshirō Ichikawa Somegorō Ichikawa Komazō Matsumoto Kingo
Kyō-ya	Nakamura Jakuemon Nakamura Shibajaku
Matsushima-ya	Kataoka Nizaemon Kataoka Gatō Kataoka Hidetarō Kataoka Shinnosuke Kataoka Ainosuke Kataoka Takatarō Kataoka Roen Kataoka Jūzō Kataoka Kamezō
Mikawa-ya	Ichikawa Danzō Ichikawa Ginnosuke
Miyoshi-ya	Kamimura Kichiya
Nakamura-ya	Nakamura Kankurō Nakamura Kantarō Nakamura Shichinosuke
Narikoma-ya	Nakamura Utaemon Nakamura Shikan Nakamura Fukusuke Nakamura Hashinosuke Nakamura Ganjirō Nakamura Kanjaku Nakamura Senjaku Nakamura Tamatarō Nakamura Umenosuke Nakamura Baijaku
Narita-ya	Ichikawa Danjūrō Ichikawa Shinnosuke
Omodaka-ya	Ichikawa Ennosuke Ichikawa Danshirō Ichikawa Kamejirō Ichikawa Ukon Ichikawa Emiya
Otowa-ya	Onoe Kikugorō Onoe Kikunosuke Onoe Tatsunosuke Onoe Matsusuke Bandō Hikosaburō Bandō Shōnosuke Bandō Kamesaburō Bandō Kametoshi
Tachibana-ya	Ichimura Uzaemon Ichimura Manjirō Ichimura Kakitsu Ichimura Tsuruzō
Takasago-ya	Nakamura Baigyoku
Takashima-ya	Ichikawa Sadanji Ichimura Unosuke
Takino-ya	Ichikawa Monnosuke
Tennōji-ya	Nakamura Tomijūrō
Teshima-ya	Arashi Keishi
Yamato-ya	Bandō Mitsugorō Bandō Tamasaburō Bandō Kichiya Bandō Shūchō Bandō Yajūrō Iwai Hanshirō
Yamazaki-ya	Kawarasaki Kunitarō
Yorozu-ya	Nakamura Karoku Nakamura Tokizō Nakamura Shinjirō Nakamura Kashō Nakamura Shidō

When people in the audience applaud an actor's performance, they often call out the *yagō* of the actor, which are shown below.

THEATERS

TOKYO

KABUKI-ZA   http://www.shochiku.co.jp

4-12-15 Ginza, Chūō-ku, Tokyo   03-3541-3131

Nearest Station: Higashi Ginza (Hibiya Line, Toei Asakusa Line)
Shimbashi (JR Yamanote Line)

Tickets: Ticket Phone Shōchiku 03-5565-6000 (10:00 a.m.–6:00 p.m.)
Box Office (10:00 a.m.–6:00 p.m.)

About the Theater / Services
The Kabuki-za is the premier Kabuki theater. No other theater presents Kabuki throughout the year.
• English headphone guide (Provides commentary and explanation relating to the plot, music, actors properties, etc.)
• English-language program
• Single-show (*Makumi*; for customers who want to see just one act, ask at Box Office for one act.)

NATIONAL THEATRE   http://www.ntj.jac.go.jp

4-1 Hayabusa-chō, Chiyoda-ku, Tokyo   03-3265-7411

Nearest Station: Hanzōmon (Hanzōmon Line)
Nagatachō (Hanzōmon Line, Yūrakuchō Line)

Tickets: Telephone 03-3230-3000 (10:00 a.m.–4:00 p.m)
Box Office (10:00 a.m.–6:00 p.m.)

About the Theater / Services
Presents Kabuki performances six times a year. Kabuki introductory courses for students and beginners are held in June and July every year.
• English Headphone Guide
(Provides commentary and explanation relating to the plot, music, actors, properties, etc.)
• English-language program

SHIMBASHI EMBU-JŌ   http://www.shochiku.co.jp

6-18-2, Ginza, Chūō-ku, Tokyo   03-3541-2211

Nearest Station: Higashi Ginza (Hibiya Line, Toei Asakusa Line)
Shimbashi (JR Yamanote Line)

Tickets: Ticket Phone Shōchiku 03-5565-6000 (10:00 a.m.–6:00 p.m.)
Box Office (10:00 a.m.–6:00 p.m.)

About the Theater
Besides Kabuki, Shimpa dramas, popular plays and other shows are presented at Shimbashi Embu-jō. It is the headquarters of the Super Kabuki of Ichikawa Ennosuke.

ASAKUSA KŌKAIDŌ   http://www.shochiku.co.jp

1-38-6, Asakusa, Taitō-ku, Tokyo   03-3844-7491

Nearest Station: Asakusa (Ginza Line, Toei Asakusa Line)

Tickets: Ticket Phone Shōchiku 03-5565-6000 (10:00 a.m.–6:00 p.m.)
Box Office (10:00 a.m.–6:00 p.m.)

Hanagata Kabuki
Performances by young Kabuki stars (Hanagata Kabuki) are held every January.

Bunkamura THEATRE COCOON   http://www.bunkamura.co.jp

2-24-1 Dōgenzaka, Shibuya-ku, Tokyo   03-3477-3244

Nearest Station: Shibuya (JR Yamanote Line, Inogashira Line, Tōyoko Line, Ginza Line, Hanzōmon Line)

Cocoon Kabuki
Young actors led by Nakamura Kankurō perform classical Kabuki plays in new and realistic styles in Edo-period settings. Started in 1994, Cocoon Kabuki is presented every other year and is much appreciated by young audiences.

MITSUKOSHI THEATER   http://www.mitsukoshi.co.jp/gekijo/

On the 6th floor of Nihombashi Mitsukoshi Department Store,
1-4-1 Muromachi, Nihombashi, Chūō-ku, Tokyo   03-3274-8675

Nearest Station: Mitsukoshimae (Ginza Line, Hanzōmon Line)

Tickets: For information, call 03-3274-8675

Mitsukoshi Kabuki
This theater presented monthly Kabuki performances by young actors from 1946 to 1950. Revived in 1992, fresh and lively performances by young actors are usually given in June every year.

KYOTO

MINAMI-ZA   http://www.shochiku.co.jp

Shijō Ōhashi Higashi-zume, Higashiyama-ku, Kyoto   075-561-1155

Nearest Station: Shijō (Keihan Line), Shijōgawara (Hankyū Line)
Kyoto (JR)

Tickets: Ticket Phone Shōchiku
0570-000-489 / 06-6214-2200 (10:00 a.m.–6:00 p.m.)
Box Office (10:00 a.m.–6:00 p.m.)

Kaomise
The Minami-za located in Kyoto, where it is said Izumo no Okuni originated Kabuki in 1603. The *kaomise*, a show with an all-star cast presented in most years in November and December, is one of the annual events of Kyoto. *Sōken*, the day on which all the *maiko* of Gion are present in the audience, is a great attraction.

OSAKA

OSAKA SHŌCHIKU-ZA   http://www.shochiku.co.jp

1-9-19 Dōtombori, Chūō-ku, Osaka   06-6214-2211

Nearest Station: Namba (Midōsuji Line)

Tickets: Ticket Phone Shōchiku
0570-000-489 / 06-6214-2200 (10:00 a.m.–6:00 p.m.)
Box Office (10:00 a.m.–6:00 p.m.)

About the Theater
The center of Kansai Kabuki, the theater was remodeled in 1997. In its *funanorikomi*, in which Kabuki actors come into the theater in ships, is famous as one of the early summer attractions of Osaka.

NAGOYA

MISONO-ZA   http://www.misonoza.co.jp

1-6-14 Sakae, Naka-ku, Nagoya   052-222-8222

Nearest Station: Fushimi (Higashiyama Line)

Tickets: Telephone 052-222-1481 (10:00 a.m.–5:00 p.m.)
Box Office (10:00 a.m.–5:00 p.m.)

About the Theater
The center of public entertainment in Nagoya, the Misono-za presents Kabuki every April and October. The annual show with an all-star cast, or *Kichirei Kaomise*, which is held in October, is extremely popular.

CHŪNICHI THEATRE   http://www.chunichi.co.jp/Theatre/

Chūnichi Building, 4-4-1 Sakae, Naka-ku, Nagoya   052-263-7171

Nearest Station: Sakae (Meijō Line, Higashiyama Line),
Sakaemachi (Meitetsu Seto Line)

Tickets: Telephone 052-290-1777 (10:00 a.m.–5:00 p.m.)
Box Office (10:00 a.m.–6:00 p.m.)

Super Kabuki
This is the Nagoya home of Ichikawa Ennosuke's Super Kabuki, which is popular for its energetic productions, and appeal to the modern audiences.

KYUSHU

HAKATA-ZA   http://www.hakataza.co.jp

2-1 Shimokawabata-chō, Hakata-ku, Fukuoka   092-263-5555

Nearest Station: Nakasukawabata (subway)

Tickets: Telephone 092-263-5555 (10:00 a.m.–6:00 p.m.)
Box Office (10:00 a.m.–6:00 p.m.)

About the Theater
Founded in June 1999. Kabuki performances are customarily scheduled in February and June.

SHIKOKU

KANAMARU-ZA

1241 Kawanishi-otsu, Kotohira-chō, Nakatado-gun, Kagawa   0877-75-6714

Nearest Station: Kotohira (JR)

Tickets / Information: Telephone 0877-75-6714 / 0877-75-0088

Kompira Kabuki
The oldest theater in Japan and designated a national important cultural property. Most seats are boxes in the pit, and the revolving stage is turned manually. In spring, the reproduction of the Edo-period *Shikoku Kompira Grand Kabuki* began in 1985 and is very popular.

YAMAGUCHI

RENASSA NAGATO   http://www.urban.ne.jp/home/renassa

818-1 Senzaki, Nagato-shi, Yamaguchi   0837-26-6001

Nearest Station: Nagatoshi (JR)

Chikamatsu Kabuki
Founded in 2000 in Nagato City, the birthplace of famous Kabuki playwright Chikamatsu Monzaemon. Every year presents one to three Chikamatsu plays by the Chikamatsu-za group led by Nakamura Ganjirō.